Restoring Dignity
in Public Schools

Restoring Dignity in Public Schools

Human Rights Education in Action

Maria Hantzopoulos

TEACHERS COLLEGE PRESS

TEACHERS COLLEGE | COLUMBIA UNIVERSITY

NEW YORK AND LONDON

Published by Teachers College Press, 1234 Amsterdam Avenue, New York, NY 10027

Cover design by Sarah Martin. Artwork by Christina Kemp.

Portions of Chapter 1 are from Hantzopoulos, M. (2015). Beyond American Exceptionalism: Centering Critical Peace Education in U.S. Public School Reform. In M. Bajaj & M. Hantzopoulos (Eds.), *Peace Education: International Perspectives*. Used by permission of Bloomsbury Publishing PLC.

Portions of Chapter 2 and other data are from Hantzopoulos, M. (2012). Considering Human Rights Education as U.S. Public School Reform. Symposium: Human Rights Education Praxis. *Peace Review: A Journal of Social Justice, 24*(1), 36–45. Reprinted by permission of Taylor & Francis LLC (http://www.tandfonline.com).

Portions of Chapter 4 are from Hantzopoulos, M. (2013). Re-engaging At Risk Youth: A Case Study of an Alternative New York City High School. In C. Brock (Ed.), *Education and Disadvantaged Young People*. New York, NY: Continuum. Used by permission of Bloomsbury Publishing PLC.

Library of Congress Cataloging-in-Publication Data

Names: Hantzopoulos, Maria, author.
Title: Restoring dignity in public schools : human rights education in action
  / Maria Hantzopoulos.
Description: New York : Teachers College Press, [2016] | Includes
  bibliographical references and index.
Identifiers: LCCN 2015047291 | ISBN 9780807757420 (pbk.) | ISBN 9780807757468
  (hardcover) | ISBN 9780807774663 (ebook)
Subjects: LCSH: Human rights—Study and teaching (Secondary)—United States.
  | Urban high schools—Curricula--United States. | Transformative
  learning--United States. | Democracy and education—United States.
Classification: LCC JC571 .H34766 2016 | DDC 323.071/273—dc23
LC record available at http://lccn.loc.gov/2015047291

ISBN 978-0-8077-5742-0 (paper)
ISBN 978-0-8077-7466-3 (ebook)

Printed on acid-free paper
Manufactured in the United States of America

23 22 21 20 19 18 17 16   8 7 6 5 4 3 2 1

Contents

Acknowledgments

This book was not a sole endeavor. I am deeply indebted to many people who helped make this book possible. First and foremost, I want to thank the students, faculty, and alumni of Humanities Preparatory Academy who generously gave me their time and, in many ways, are coauthors in this undertaking. Thank you for trusting me to tell these stories, so that others can learn and be inspired by the beauty that is Prep. Special mention goes to Perry Weiner, Christina Kemp, and Vincent Brevetti, who have served as inspiring mentors and friends to me and effortlessly model passion, commitment, and love in their daily lives and in their work with youth.

Many people contributed feedback and input during the various stages of this project and I am truly appreciative of their friendship and guidance. In particular, I want to acknowledge my amazing accountability group of Dina López, Carmina Makar, Rosario Torres-Guevara, Roozbeh Shirazi, and Zeena Zakharia for their consistent love and prodding; as well as my writing group of Dana Wright, Lionel Howard, Ari Rotramel, and Emma Sterret for their brilliant feedback, sage advice, and general good-natured support. I am also thankful to the many people who offered encouragement, critical feedback, and friendship throughout this process, including in the very early stages and up until the bitter end. These people include my generous colleagues and friends at Vassar College: particularly Colette Cann, Erin McCloskey, Chris Bjork, Christine Malsbary, and Tracey Holland, as well as friends, mentors, and scholars not already named who truly have provided so much support and encouragement along the way: Monisha Bajaj, Lesley Bartlett, Tricia Callender, Cambria Dodd-Russell, Ofelia García, Ameena Ghaffar-Kucher, Brooke Harris-Garad, Tatyana Kleyn, Maureen Matarese, Mary Mendenhall, Rosa Rivera-McCutchen, Alia Tyner-Mullings, Laura Valdiviezo, Fran Vavrus, Hakim Williams, and Andria Wisler. I want to recognize my students at Vassar College, with whom many of these ideas have been discussed, shaped, shared, and challenged. There are too many of you to name, but our classes and thinking collectively around these issues has only advanced and sharpened this work. I am truly fortunate that the students in our Education Department are some of the most critically engaged people on campus.

Tawnya Fay Switzer receives a stand-alone mention for her stellar and superior editing skills; thank you tremendously for being so diligent, patient, flexible, and attentive! I am also fortunate and appreciative of the hard work and critical eyes of my wonderful research assistants during this project: Hannah Reynolds, Eunice Roh, and David Pham. Finally, I am thankful for the feedback from the editors at Teachers College Press, particularly Brian Ellerbeck, who believed in this project from the beginning, as well as Lori Tate, whose feedback helped strengthen the work. Thank you!

Financially, this book, at different stages, was supported by the following grants and fellowships: The Spencer Foundation Research Training Grant, The Teachers College Office of Policy and Research Fellowship, the Coalition of Essential Schools Theodore Sizer Scholars Grant, the Tatlock Endowed Fund for Strategic Faculty Support, and the Jane Rosenthal Heimerdinger Fund. I also owe so much to the caregivers who loved and looked after my children so I could finish this book; in particular I would like to mention Eleni Papastefanou, Irini Zora, and the teachers at Les Enfants Montessori and P.S. 300Q in Astoria, Queens.

Finally, I would like to acknowledge and express appreciation to my family, including my parents, Peter and Chris, and all of my siblings, for their incessant love and support. I also owe so much to my partner, Johnny Farraj, and my children Dalia and Ziyad, who not only push me to be my best self, but love and encourage me anyway, even when I fall short. Thank you for your love and patience.

CHAPTER 1

(Re)Framing Urban Schools
Beyond Accountability, Discipline, and Punishment in Urban Educational Reform

Prep was the most amazing experience. . . . I think it changed my perspective on life and what my potential as a human being is in this world. I don't think I could have gotten that from any other alternative school or from any other high school period. (Queenia, interview, May 2007)

Mainstream media and common narratives that circulate about young people in urban schools often depict them as disengaged, apathetic, and ultimately disinterested in schooling. Yet, when I began to interview and collect data from students at Humanities Preparatory Academy (Prep) about their experiences with participatory forms of education at their school, I was somewhat overwhelmed by the sheer joy and positivity they expressed. Although remembrance can be tinged with romanticized nostalgia, I was particularly struck by the specific ways Queenia and other former students described Prep as a school that was not just intellectually challenging, but also transformative and pivotal in shaping their outlook and approach to life. While clearly there are multiple factors that affect the world-view of students, these testimonies undoubtedly show that school very much mattered to these young people while they attended and even after they left. Although I always pushed those I was interviewing to think more critically about their experiences, students and alumni inevitably reframed their critiques to make sure that I understood the positive—both to testify to the school's impact and to declare that the school should never, ever go away.

Students and alumni often made comments like the quote that opened this chapter, shedding light on the ways they made meaning of their experiences at this small, slightly run-down, often unheard of public alternative school in lower Manhattan. While they always described being intellectually challenged, they invariably spoke just as passionately about how the humanizing and democratizing school culture profoundly impacted their adolescent and adult lives. In this sense, the intellectual rigor and the participatory culture are not separate processes, but two essential threads that weave together to center the humanity and dignity of young people in this space.

1

Nonetheless, we find ourselves in a climate where high-stakes testing, accountability, punitive action, and the privatization of public schooling dominate educational policy in the United States. Couched in policies and language of standards, choice, accountability, and punishment, these approaches have had profound implications for the lives of young people in schools. Although much is known about sound educational methods, ideas, and practices that promote the development of the whole person, government-sponsored reforms situate these approaches as supplementary to "the basics" and tend to ignore them altogether. By creating mandates that focus solely on test scores and narrow conceptions of learning and discipline, policymakers often overlook various factors, such as overall school culture, that may improve schools and address inequities in schooling (American Federation of Teachers Racial Justice Task Force, 2015). As a result, completely absent from policy equations are the pedagogical practices and structures that (re)socialize students academically and equip them with the tools to succeed in school and live meaningful lives. The consequences of these omissions are hardly innocuous, particularly as empirical research continually shows that educational policies in the past 15 years have only exacerbated the achievement and opportunities gap, especially among poor students and students of color (Arbuthnot, 2011; Berliner & Glass, 2014; McNeil, Coppola, Radigan, & Vazquez-Heilig, 2011; Ravitch, 2014). In contrast to what happens at Prep, these policies ultimately function to dehumanize and deny dignity to young people and their teachers.

This book presents an alternative view to the dominant discourses, which demonize public schools and suggest that reform must come by way of increased testing, privatization, and disciplinary control. *I assert that an approach centered on the dignity of students and teachers is essential in and must drive any efforts at public school reform.* Specifically, I contend that a comprehensive approach to human rights education (HRE) in schools is one possible antidote to the current educational policy discourses and practices that erase the realities of vibrant and engaging public schools. I argue that public schools are sites of possibility and urge policymakers to move past prevailing policies of reform and to incorporate holistic strategies that truly benefit children. By featuring thriving schools that enact HRE, I draw attention to the possibilities of this form of education as a means to promote democratization and active citizenship through the creation of more humane schooling environments.

While I ground the book with examples of public schools that position dignity at the core of their missions, the bulk of my argument and analysis is based on ethnographic research conducted at Humanities Preparatory Academy, a small public high school in New York City. Drawing from rich narratives that foreground youth experiences, I illuminate the policies and practices of HRE in action and show how schools can intentionally create an environment in which a culture of dignity, respect, tolerance, and democracy flourishes. By showing how these schools (re)socialize students who have been "left behind" by current market-based strategies and centralized approaches to educational reform, the book highlights a paradigm alternative to the currently favored strategies of increased testing, privatization, and disciplinary control.

My analysis derives from 2 years of interviews, observation, and ethnographic research at Prep; my prior experiences teaching in the school for 10 years; and my familiarity with and involvement in various New York City educational reform movements of the past 20 years. I provide a rationale and model for HRE praxis in schools by interweaving the complex accounts and experiences of students and teachers at Prep with the practices at multiple HRE-centric schools. I argue that HRE is not supplemental or secondary to other educational initiatives; instead, it is threaded into the fabric of all aspects of curriculum and school life. While sometimes this thread gets frayed and pulled in different directions, I argue that through their commitment to these practices, schools inevitably grapple with the messy and often contradictory processes of democratic schooling to create humanized spaces that center the dignity of every person. This book explores how Prep operationalizes HRE through its unique processes and structures, thereby illuminating how the school becomes a fertile ground for learning, especially for those most disenchanted with school. These illustrative and empirically supported examples show how such strategies work to benefit young people and redress the systemic and structural injustices that currently pervade our educational landscape, repositioning public schools as potential sites of possibility and hope.

CURRENT OBSTACLES TO EQUITABLE EDUCATIONAL REFORM

In the past 2 decades, public discourse in the United States about "failing" public schools has permeated the urban educational landscape, paving the way for macro-level policy reforms ostensibly designed to improve schools. Tied to accountability strategies that intend to increase student achievement, initiatives such as No Child Left Behind, Race to the Top, and the Common Core State Standards not only measure student progress by performance on high-stakes standardized tests, but also rank and evaluate teachers, schools, and districts based on these very same indicators. These policies have always been met with criticism and controversy, but their proliferation on national, state, and local levels has been unstoppable. Shaped by rhetoric that demonizes public schools and their teachers and students, these policies often are seen as the "commonsense" approach to remediating failure in the public eye (Apple, 2005; Hantzopoulos & Shirazi, 2014; Kumashiro, 2008). Implicit in the discourses surrounding these policies is that public schools are presently incapable of preparing and educating children. Thus, those most active in shaping policy in the past 15 years are rarely educators; they are often business professionals, politicians, and self-proclaimed reformers who made their careers in education but spent little time in schools and classrooms. Often citing statistics that point to the under-preparedness of U.S. youth, these reformers push policies that seemingly raise standards through benchmarks, test scores, and an overall discourse of accountability. Embedded with neoliberal free-market principles, these policies reflect faith in the idea that competition, innovation, and accountability will drive students and schools to perform better (see Apple, 2005; Hursh, 2007; Lipman, 2011).

Overwhelming evidence, however, points to how these reforms, in reality, have been the real failure (see Berliner & Biddle, 1995; Berliner & Glass, 2014; D'Agastino, 2012; McCarty, 2010; Ravitch, 2011, 2014). By placing primacy on test scores and school performance above all other educational matters, these initiatives create pressure on teachers and schools to prepare students solely for the tests—at the expense of other empirically sound and effective pedagogies. This emphasis on "accountability" through high-stakes exams has only exacerbated existing inequities, particularly for those who historically have been marginalized from schooling, including students of color, low-income students, multilingual students, and those with diagnosed disabilities (Amrein & Berliner, 2003; Arbuthnot, 2011; Au, 2009; Futrell & Rotberg, 2002; Haywood, 2002; C. Horn, 2003; Katsyianis, Zhang, Ryan, & Jones, 2007; Marchant, 2004; Maudaus & Clarke, 2001; McNeil, 2005; McNeil et al., 2011; Menken, 2008; Vazquez-Heilig & Darling-Hammond, 2008). While a variety of factors (including cultural biases, language ability, access to supplementary resources, etc.) negatively affect student performance on these tests, studies repeatedly have shown that marginalized populations are more vulnerable to not completing high school and also that the "achievement gap" has widened with increased testing policies that place pressure on students and teachers (see Bridgeland, Dilulio, & Balfanz, 2009; Bridgeland, Dilulio, & Morison, 2006; McNeil et al., 2011).

Furthermore, narrow emphasis on testing has risen alongside the proliferation of demoralizing and punitive school climates that contribute to pushing students out of school, particularly in schools with zero-tolerance disciplinary policies that punish students for minor infractions. Research shows that a history of suspension from school increases a student's likelihood of dropping out by 78% (Lee, Cornell, Gregory, & Fan, 2011; Suh & Suh, 2007). Moreover, scholars like Fine (1991), Bowditch (1993), and Fergusen (2001) have ethnographically shown ways in which students, particularly young people of color, often are in fact framed in school environments and in some cases criminalized and constructed as "trouble." Because studies repeatedly show that schools with excessively punitive disciplinary policies and high suspension rates have higher dropout rates (see Christie, Jolivette, & Nelson, 2007; Suh & Suh, 2007), many scholars and youth advocates prefer the term "pushed out" to describe the phenomenon of students leaving school. Tuck (2012) uses this term in her work, but also shows how some students are uncomfortable with this label because it suggests lack of agency and being duped.

While student behavior certainly contributes to disciplinary measures like suspension, several reports and studies show that school climate, culture, and policies may unnecessarily increase suspension rates and contribute to pushing students out of school. In other words, the systems and structures in place create an unwelcoming environment for students in school. For instance, the National Economic and Social Rights Initiative (2007), American Civil Liberties Union (2010), New York Civil Liberties Union, Make the Road, and Annenberg Institute of School Reform (2009), and Independent Commission on Public Education (2012) have all published reports revealing that New York City students are disproportionately subjected to degrading treatment in the classroom, unfair disciplinary policies, and a threatening police and security presence. A recent brief jointly prepared by the African American Forum and the Columbia University Law School Center for Intersectionality and Social Policy Studies shows the impact of such policies on girls of color (Crenshaw, 2015). For instance, one case includes the handcuffed arrest of a 12-year-old Latina in Queens for doodling on a desk (Monahan, 2010). There has been national outrage most recently over a young Black woman being slammed down and dragged out of a classroom by a White male school security agent caught on video by her classmates. Apparently, she was simply not participating in class that day. Her friend that video-taped the horror was also arrested. While these may seem like extreme examples, students interviewed in the aforementioned reports indicate that this type of humiliating and violent treatment is all too commonplace in schools.

Rather than creating safer schools, these punitive measures have created hostile learning environments. As mentioned, students who frequently are disciplined or suspended from school are much more likely to not complete high school. Moreover, "zero-tolerance" discipline policies often work in tandem with high-stakes testing; the former criminalize students for minor infractions of school rules, and the latter forces administrators to push out low-performing students to improve their school's overall test scores (Advancement Project et al., 2011; American Civil Liberties Union, 2010). While research also shows that individual, social, cultural, psychological, and economic variables contribute to dropout patterns (Rumberger, 2004), the studies mentioned articulate the importance of school culture on the retention and attainment rate of students in school. Tuck's (2012) work deftly shows how such structures create "humiliating ironies" for students that propel their disengagement, and eventual departure, from school.

"Accountability" reform has become high-stakes for both students and schools as students' failure to meet specific achievement targets has resulted in drastic administrative and curricular changes and loss of school funding, and now is linked to the ways that teachers' performance is evaluated (see Karp, 2006).[1] Consequently, many schools and districts manipulate results to mask the realities of their students' achievements on these tests (Nichols & Berliner, 2007).[2] These policies, couched in accountability, have thus polarized debates surrounding the future of public education in the United States, and many argue that these policies are linked to attempts to privatize public education. For instance, in urban centers like New York City, Philadelphia, New Orleans, and Chicago, many schools that do not produce enough students at achievement level are deemed "failing" and are slated for school closure or complete takeover. Often, this paves the way for the creation of charter and specialized schools in these spaces, which many suggest are a covert attempt to dismantle public education. While some charter and specialized schools certainly have been instrumental in serving and providing for underserved communities, as a whole these alternatives have not proven to be any more successful than public schools (Center for Research on Educational Outcomes [CREDO], 2009; Ravitch, 2014). Yet, their proliferation in the past several years has been astounding, particularly as public discourse frames them as a panacea for school reform (see Fabricant & Fine, 2012).

Overall, the fabrication of "failure" and crisis that catalyzes these reforms in fact produces and generates more failure. Several scholars have been documenting the ways that these processes work together to erode the public good and bolster private industry, which in recent years has led to growing opposition at a broad-based grassroots level (Fabricant & Fine, 2012; Hagopian, 2014; Lipman, 2011; Meier, 2000; Neil, 2015; Ravitch, 2011, 2014; Schniedewind & Sapon-Shevin, 2012; Watkins, 2012). Yet, despite documentation of and resistance to these negative outcomes, overtesting, over-policing, and privatization in schools permeate the broader school reform agenda in the United States. In a poignant blogpost, Taubman (2013) captured this phenomenon succinctly:

> It is no longer enough to list the mind-numbing effects of high-stakes tests or reveal how teachers' hard-won knowledge about kids, schools and curriculum has been replaced with a fanatical faith in the free market and the bottom line. Scholarly research, numerous studies, and reasoned argument have not prevailed over those who scream crisis, substitute test score gaps for income gaps, and blame unions, teachers and non-charter public schools for the nation's ills. Nor have we halted the transformation by exposing the profit motive behind so many of the educational reforms. And although we must persevere, it's not enough to describe how these reforms have turned public education into a grim, wasteland littered with mediocre charter schools, a wasteland where teaching, at least in the hands of "innovators" like Doug Lemov, author of *Teach Like a Champion: 49 Techniques that Put Students on the Path to College,* resembles

dog training, and curriculum and learning are reduced to test prep. These strategies are not working. We need to be more ruthless in our resistance.

As Taubman aptly elucidates, the documentation of these failed and harmful policies and the collective clamor to reverse and interrupt them needs to continue, but further strategizing is necessary in order to reverse these harmful trends because they have been so deeply sewn into the new educational policy fabric.

HUMAN DIGNITY AS AN APPROACH TO SCHOOL REFORM
AND EDUCATIONAL EQUITY

In response to over-policing and over-testing in schools, youth and educational activists have begun to demand a human rights framework to education. For instance, the National Economic and Social Rights Initiative has been incredibly active in their push to reframe education with a human rights lens that "includes not only teaching essential academic knowledge and skills, but also creating a positive school environment, supporting the emotional and behavioral development of young people, and encouraging students to participate in developing the school policies that impact their education" (Sullivan, 2007, p. 45). In this sense, human rights education must go beyond classroom content and permeate the whole school. As noted by Felisa Tibbits (2008), human rights education historically has been "primarily focused on teaching and learning," and should "eventually [be] seen as part of an overall 'human rights based approach' to schooling, which calls attention to overall school culture, policies, and practices related to human rights values" (p. 2). By incorporating a holistic and schoolwide approach to HRE, Amnesty International (2012) posits that students will assimilate a culture of human rights, so "all members of a given community understand, value and protect human rights, where the values of equality, dignity, respect, non-discrimination and participation anchor policies and processes within the community" (p. 3). Collectively, these approaches provide a framework to understand how schools might institutionalize pervasive forms of HRE and create a climate of dignity for the young people who have been most marginalized by the inequities and injustices of American schooling. In the context of New York City, where the opportunities gap remains wide among youth—based on race, class, language, and (dis)ability—HRE can serve as a source of academic (re)socialization and dropout prevention, in addition to a source of human rights learning.

In this spirit, *Restoring Dignity in Public Schools* is an illustrative counternarrative to the mainstream discourses of "failing" public schools in the United States, contributing to this conversation a picture of the possibilities of public schools that implement HRE in action. A growing number of recently published books and studies show the practices of exemplary urban public schools, illustrating how concepts such as strong student–teacher relationships, positive school culture, and engaging academic curricula can improve and address inequities in U.S. schooling (Antrop-Gonzalez, 2011; Bartlett & García, 2011; De Jesús, 2012; Hantzopoulos & Tyner-Mullings, 2012; Knoester, 2012; Rivera-McCutchen, 2012; Rodriguez & Conchas, 2008; Tyner-Mullings, 2014). *Restoring Dignity in Public Schools,* however, is unique in that it situates school practices in a larger human rights education framework. In this book, I am attentive to the ways that school actors implement a pervasive schoolwide curriculum that both validates students' humanity and worth, and teaches students to do the same to others, exemplifying the praxis of HRE. As scholars in the field increasingly argue, HRE must go beyond what content is learned and taught in the classroom and be applied in a more comprehensive manner (see Hantzopoulos, 2012a; Tibbits, 2008).

This book, therefore, shows how a holistic approach beyond the classroom might be operationalized to become pervasive on a macro school level. Through pragmatic descriptions and textured accounts of quotidian experiences of students and teachers who experience HRE, I illuminate how school actors engage with the distinctive practices and philosophies of their schools and make meaning of their experiences at institutions committed not only to traditional academic and college preparation, but also to a world that is more peaceful, democratic, and just. Since little scholarship attends to the enactment of holistic human rights and participatory practices in public schools, this book addresses questions posed by scholars seeking empirical studies that examine localized understandings of participant experiences in schools that have put HRE into action (see Bajaj, 2008).

While prominent human rights education scholars like Bajaj (2011, 2012), Flowers (2004), and Tibbits (2002, 2008) demonstrate how HRE can foster attitudes of tolerance, respect, and solidarity within and beyond the school community, as well as increase student social and political engagement, I contend that HRE also can serve as a form of academic (re) socialization by motivating young people to stay and do well in school. Since a full-scale human rights approach to education engages young people as actors in their own learning, the process is equally as important as the outcome, which is the learning and inculcation of human rights values. In this sense, HRE can serve as a valid and necessary part of public school revitalization and reform, and this book aims to shift current conversations about HRE in new directions more tightly linked to educational access, attainment, and success.

While HRE, and its link to human dignity, often is theorized (see Reardon, 1996; Tibbits, 1996), practitioners, educators, and scholars frequently want to understand how it operates in practice. In this book, I argue that schools must cultivate a culture of *care, respect, critical questioning,* and *participation* in order to build school environments that are anchored in human dignity and worth, as these approaches have been empirically documented to engage students academically, intellectually, socially, and emotionally in their school environments (see Antrop-Gonzalez, 2011; Bajaj, 2009, 2012; Bartlett & García, 2011; Bartlett & Koyama, 2012; De Jesús, 2012; Hantzopoulos, 2011b, 2012a, 2012b; Rivera-McCutchen, 2012; Rodriguez & Conchas, 2008; Tyner-Mullings, 2012, 2014; Winn, 2007). By uniting these approaches under a synthesized human rights rubric, I provide a framework for schools and school leaders to both institutionalize a pervasive form of HRE and create a climate of dignity for young people, particularly for those most underserved by American schools.

SCHOOL CONTEXTS AND METHODS

The book is grounded with examples of public schools in NYC that center human dignity at the core of their missions and practices. As a former high school teacher and staff developer in New York City public schools, I have worked extensively with many schools, within New York City and nationwide, that utilize in some form the core principles and practices of HRE. My experience as a mentor liaison for the Coalition of Essential Schools Small Schools Network and my participation in the New York Performance Standards Consortium (Consortium), as both a former teacher and current principal investigator on a research project documenting the transition of Regents-based schools into project-based assessment schools, have provided me keen insight into the broader reform landscape and deepened my knowledge of effective schooling in New York City. Drawing from several years of experience as a practitioner and teacher educator working in Prep and similar schools in the Consortium network, I illuminate the policies and practices of HRE in action at several school sites. Many of the examples of school practices in the book are drawn from Consortium schools such as Urban Academy, the James Baldwin School, and El Puente Academy for Peace and Justice. While these schools do not necessarily name their practices as HRE, much of what they do aligns with HRE principles (further explored in Chapter 2).

The thrust of my argument and analysis, however, is based on ethnographic research conducted at Humanities Preparatory Academy, where I taught for many years prior to conducting research there. Conceived as a program in a larger school for students who were underserved and potentially at risk for dropping out, Prep was founded to both engage these students in their learning and rigorously prepare them for college. Due to significant success with this population, the program gradually expanded, and 4 years later, Prep became an autonomous public school. While the school now serves a mixed population of students who have had previous "success" in schools and students who have struggled, Prep has maintained a distinct learning environment that, according to the school mission, attempts to (re)engage all students "by personalizing our learning situations, by democratizing and humanizing the school environment, and by creating a 'talking culture,' an atmosphere of informal intellectual discourse among students and faculty" (Appendix B).Thus, by constructing a radically alternative educational environment rooted in democracy, public intellectualism, and a caring school culture, Prep presents itself as a place that provides a transformative and liberating experience for its students within and beyond the sphere of schooling. According to the mission, Prep endeavors to uphold these core values and create a space for students to "find their voices" and "speak knowledgeably and thoughtfully on issues that concern their school, their world" (see Appendix B).

The school serves a population that spans the socioeconomic, racial, and ethnic spectra of the city, and thus remains representative of an integrated educational space, while many other urban public schools are de facto segregated by race and class (Hannah-Jones, 2015; Kucsera, 2014). At the time of my original research (2005–2008), the self-identified racial background of the student body was as follows: 40% Latino, 38% Black, 12% White, 6% Asian, and 4% Other; 12% of the student population was enrolled in special education and 62% qualified for free or reduced-price lunch. In 2014, the student population was 57% Latino, 28% Black, 9% White, 4% Asian, and 3% Other; 12% were enrolled in special education and 74% qualified for free lunch (see insideschools.org). Prep's student heterogeneity reveals the potential for actual diverse integration in urban schools. Similarly, at the time of my research and at present, the teaching staff represented the diversity found in the student body.

While words like *diversity* and *urban youth* are most certainly often code words to describe low-income students of color (see Hantzopoulos & Tyner-Mullings, 2012; Tuck, 2012), the usages of these words in this book are more expansive to complicate singular assumptions to which *urban* and *diverse* often refer. Tuck (2012) explains that *urban* (much like the word *diversity*) are ways to "talk about race without having to talk about race" (p. 12). She and others "rescue the word urban from color-blind discourse" to center the racialized processes in urban contexts that simultaneously privilege White bodies at the expense, underdevelopment, and dispossession of Black and Brown ones (see Anyon et. al., 2009; Fine & Ruglis, 2009; Tuck, 2012). Schools, for instance, are shaped by these processes in a variety of ways, including through stark urban segregation that leads to abundantly resourced (middle-income White) schools and underresourced (low-income, predominantly Black and Brown) schools in the same city.

In my previous work with Tyner-Mullings (2012), we agree and also argue that discourses around *urban* can also be reframed to embody meanings ideas about community, social justice, and participation, particularly with regard to schooling. This more robust understanding necessarily rests on shifting away from deficit views of urban life; it considers what is possible and in fact existent when communities band together from within and across difference. Since Prep exemplifies an integrated space across raced, classed, and socioeconomic lines, the school also illustrates the complexities of what words like *urban* and *diversity* actually mean. This commitment to heterogeneity is a key feature of Prep, intentionally valued as a means by which to interrupt the segregated processes that often define urban schools. Further, this commitment is not color or context blind, but rather one that engages difference to imagine new vibrant communities across multiracial lines (see also Fine, Weis, & Powell, 1997; Hantzopoulos & Tyner-Mullings, 2012).

In this context, Prep is considered a successful school because its graduation and college acceptance rates are well above average for a New York City public school. For example, Prep has averaged 91 to 100% college acceptance rates from the time it opened as a school in 1997 through the time of my fieldwork; the citywide rate did not rise above 62% during that same period (New York Performance Standards Consortium, 2008). The dropout rate remains below 4%, compared with the city rate of 19.9%, despite the fact that Prep accepts many students who have been pushed out of other schools and turn to Prep as their last chance. These figures demonstrate the school's commitment to addressing larger structural racial and economic inequalities embedded within the NYC education system.

Prep's radically re-conceptualized approach to schooling reflects an HRE framework that rethinks the form, content, and structure of traditional schooling. From its inception, Prep has remained steadfast in its commitment to student-centered education, critical pedagogy, and the school's Core Values of peace, justice, democracy, and respect for humanity, intellect, truth, and diversity. According to teachers interviewed, these foci undergird classroom and school community practices. One way this happens is through the flattened hierarchy of school governance—staff, parents, and students are invited to create and shape school policy and practices. While there is a school principal and teacher co-director, there are rotating leadership positions, student advisory councils, and consensus-based decision-making. With fewer than 200 students, the school remains relatively small for a NYC public high school.

The school has reframed how students are grouped academically to interrupt how traditional tracking in schools perpetuates inequalities and structural violence (Galtung, 2008; Haavelsrud, 2008; Oakes, 2005); classes are de-tracked, mixed-age, and heterogeneously grouped. For most classes, there are no prerequisites based on grade levels, prior achievement, or ability. Students choose classes based on interest and meet with an advisor to ensure that their choices fulfill both the state distribution requirements and student-set academic goals. Prep is also unique in that it has a waiver from the Regents exams, the standardized high-stakes subject tests used to graduate students in New York State. Instead, Prep uses a form of assessment known as performance-based assessment, which resembles the college- or graduate-level thesis system (see Foote, 2012; Hantzopoulos, 2009). This type of assessment has allowed for the creation of thematic courses, building off students' interests and questions they have about the world. Accordingly, classes often reflect themes in peace and social justice education, as well as enduring questions for humanity at large.

Finally, Prep has many nonacademic participatory structures that support learning, critical dialogue, and democratic engagement. These include Advisory, Town Meeting and Quads, and the Fairness Committee, all of which are part of the school day and are built into the overall schedule. Advisory is a daily class period, capped at 15 students, in which students not only discuss issues that often are expanded upon in Town Meeting, but also receive academic support, develop leadership skills, and build community with the other members of their group. Town Meeting, which is a weekly whole-school gathering where students and teachers discuss a myriad of personal, community, schoolwide, national, and global issues, is also an integral space for discussion and debate. Prep is also one of a few schools in New York City that actively use a form of restorative justice, known as the Fairness Committee, as a means to address and discuss infractions in the community (Hantzopoulos, 2011a, 2013). While other New York City schools are starting to adopt restorative justice models through the work of the Dignity in Schools Campaign and Teachers Unite, Prep pioneered this approach by having the Fairness Committee in place since inception. It is often in these spaces that students can influence and implement schoolwide policy through a direct democratic model and emphasis on critical dialogue and healthy debate.

Throughout the book, I draw from data collected at Prep to illustrate how the school promotes humanistic values and ultimately provides a comprehensive form of human rights education, foregrounding youth and educator experience. The data were collected mostly at Prep between 2006 and 2008, but also include follow-up interviews with alumni and school workers that took place between 2008 and 2014 (see Appendix A for demographic info). The data collection process included participant observation at the school; interviews with former and current students, teachers, and administrators; and anecdotal surveys. In particular, I draw from descriptive field-notes to illustrate how school actors enact critical pedagogy and democratic approaches to schooling, in addition to promoting the school's humanistic values, to provide a comprehensive form of human rights education.

Although they, too, have a student demographic largely comprising young people who have been disproportionately underserved, the other schools mentioned in this book also maintain higher graduation and college acceptance rates and lower dropout rates through models that use HRE practices. For instance, based on information gathered from the NYC Department of Education databases, Consortium schools serve students of color, students with disabilities, and English language learners at higher rates than NYC public schools at large; at the same time, Consortium students graduate and subsequently attend and persist in college at much higher rates (New York Performance Standards Consortium, 2013). Thus, in the context of New York City, where the opportunities gap remains wide among youth based on race, class, language, and (dis)ability, HRE principles in schools counteract mainstream educational policy discourses and practices, and can serve as a model for responsive urban educational reform. The research at Prep specifically reveals that HRE was pivotal to students' positive experience at school. Students cite the importance of strong intergenerational relationships between young people and adults, as well as the intentional Core Values framework that infuses all aspects of school life and the culturally relevant, inquiry- and project-based curriculum (as shown in Chapters 4, 5, and 6). Moreover, students appreciate and value the participatory spaces in the school that foster critical dialogue and engagement among the overall school population. Past and present students suggest that these spaces and structures contributed to their understandings of democracy, sense of agency, and perceived ability to initiate change. Overall, they mention that these structures helped them feel part of a community, find their voice, and critically question the world, suggesting that Prep catalyzed them to participate actively in decisionmaking in school and beyond school (as shown in Chapters 6, 7, and 8). As a result, many students, including those who felt marginalized and silenced in previous school settings, found refuge and acceptance at Prep. I highlight various ways by which teachers enacted this form of education, opening a window into the practices of effective teaching in urban schools.

The book emphasizes how Prep enacts an organic form of HRE in the context of New York City, which both provides a rationale for this type of education and presents a model for HRE praxis not only in urban public schools, but in American public schools in general. While the school does not explicitly call its approach HRE, the key tenets of the school's mission and practices line up with the aims and goals of HRE. The data show that this approach is not supplemental or secondary to other educational initiatives; instead, it is woven into the fabric of all aspects of curriculum and school life. As a result, readers can expect to gain a deep understanding of how Prep operationalizes HRE through its unique democratic and student-inclusive processes and structures, and thereby creates a fertile ground for learning, especially for those most disenchanted with school. By juxtaposing the practices of Prep with the practices of other successful public schools that also employ participatory, student-centered, and welcoming school strategies, I demonstrate the sweeping promise and possibility of enacting HRE in public schools throughout urban centers in the United States.

CHAPTER ROADMAP

The remainder of the book illustratively shows how HRE serves as a means for public school reform, since it not only fosters human rights learning, but also serves as a mechanism to include students who have been demoralized by school. Chapter 2 reviews the history and emergence of human rights education globally, and argues for ways that HRE should be considered in a localized U.S. and NYC context. Specifically, I unpack the myriad approaches to and definitions of HRE and argue that in an urban public school setting, HRE necessarily must focus on local community issues and connect these to larger patterns. In this sense, I theoretically link HRE to scholarship on democratic education, critical pedagogy, and peace education, to collectively yield a comprehensive form of HRE that is attentive to participatory processes, skills, social action, and an overall school culture that engages students as transformative agents in school. Grounded in concepts of agency, liberation, and subjectivity, I show how ultimately HRE is centered on participating in and creating a humanized culture of dignity for and among students and teachers. I build off three different frameworks developed by Amnesty International, the National Economic and Social Rights Initiative, and the Independent Commission on Public Education in New York City to situate the study and describe how this may transpire in schools.

Chapter 3 explores why the key components of HRE (a culture of *care, respect, critical questioning,* and *participation*) are essential in building a school environment that is anchored in human dignity and worth, further making the case for placing HRE at the forefront of school reform. Specifically, I focus on the stark differences between mainstream urban schools and those that enact aspects of HRE, to illustrate the need for the latter approach. This framing sets the groundwork for the remainder of the book, which emphasizes more specifically how schools can enact HRE, and especially these aforementioned aspects of school culture, by offering specific strategies and approaches used by several NYC schools.

Chapter 4 illuminates the qualities of care and, more specifically, the ways that strong student–teacher relationships can help build a culture of human dignity and worth in public schools. While plenty of current research describes the importance of student–teacher relationships in addressing inequities in schooling, Chapter 4 advances these conversations and addresses a current gap in the literature by placing youth perspectives at the center, giving attention to how students describe and understand these relationships.

Chapter 5 illustrates the importance of "respect" in centering human dignity in schools and suggests how this aspect of HRE can be operationalized in school practice. While positive student–teacher relationships are built and formed even in hostile school climates, I argue that explicit values-oriented frameworks and intentionality about school space can facilitate more humanizing and democratizing intellectual and social interactions among peers and adults. To support my argument, I show how students at Prep view the school's Core Values and the unique space of Prep Central (a common student-teacher workspace) as essential to their schooling experience, and how this helped infuse respect among the heterogeneous and intergenerational members of the school community, ultimately contributing to a sense of belonging, tolerance, community, recognition, and self-worth among the student body.

In Chapter 6, I show how academic curricula can center human dignity in schools by shedding light on the intentional curriculum approaches that define most classrooms at Prep. These approaches—namely inclusive conversation, inquiry-based design, culturally and socially relevant content, heterogeneous groupings, and project-based work—all help advance the principles and goals of HRE, which include a culture of critical questioning, public intellectualism, student agency, and social change. Furthermore, HRE is a framework that intellectually invigorates and challenges students, and most alumni from schools that enact HRE feel extremely confident about actively engaging in their discussion-based social science and humanities classes in college. On the flip side, I highlight some concerns regarding the quality of Prep's constructivist, student-centered math programs, as some alumni questioned whether the program was sufficiently rigorous for college preparation. Because this tension points to deeper questions about potential academic weaknesses of HRE, I offer suggestions and strategies that might help schools and teachers prepare students for all facets of postsecondary work and schooling without compromising the constructivist nature of HRE programming.

Chapter 7 highlights another major strategy to make human dignity a pivotal aspect of school reform: the role of nonacademic participatory spaces for democratic engagement. Coupled with the curriculum described in Chapter 6, efforts to engage students as participatory actors in the school environment contribute to a culture of critical consciousness and agency, a culture that is fundamental and necessary to institutionalize an HRE framework in schools. Spaces like Advisory, Town Meetings/Quads, and the Fairness Committee provide room for transformative agency, allow students to cultivate their "voice" and explore new ways of thinking about complex issues and their role in the world, and challenge them to actively approach individual growth and structural change. I focus mostly on Prep, but also provide examples from other schools that approach curriculum design and use participatory spaces in similar ways, to briefly illuminate how nonacademic participatory spaces for democratic engagement might be envisioned at various schooling locales.

In Chapter 8, I consider the role of HRE in students' lives within and beyond school, and offer insight and recommendations to help schools and educators assist many students as they navigate transitions and complex social realms. While students leaving HRE-centered schools generally intend to change society, work toward dismantling unjust structures, or simply give back to their communities in some way, they also brush up against realities that challenge their assumptions about their ability to actually effect change and voice opinions. This friction is particularly pronounced when young people must contend with power dynamics and larger structural inequities that inhibit their sense of agency within and beyond the school. Nonetheless, I argue that while students sometimes feel restricted by what they are able to do in these situations, their words and actions suggest that many of these young people also find creative ways to reclaim their voices and maintain hope. I ultimately maintain that schools that use a holistic HRE framework are manifestations of sites in which (and by which) agency is negotiated, contested, and remade, often in unexpected, unassuming, and contradictory ways, and that there is much to be learned from this process. I close the chapter by highlighting multiple strategies schools can employ to help students reconcile the social worlds they do and will navigate, and I provide substantive suggestions for schools to help students negotiate this transition more effectively.

The conclusion, Chapter 9, reiterates the importance of establishing a humanized school culture that centers the dignity of students and teachers in all public school reform efforts. I argue that this includes an emphasis on building a culture of care, respect, critical questioning, and participation, undergirded by and aligned with a human rights educational framework. Through their enactment of curricula that validate and value students' humanity and teach these young people to respect and value others, Prep and the other schools featured in this volume exemplify the praxis of human rights education. While present educational policies narrowly focus on testing and discipline despite evidence that these initiatives have only exacerbated inequities in schooling, I posit that mainstreaming HRE offers hope that public schools can work toward further educational access and attainment. Overall, these schools offer an instructive source of inspiration to see not only how HRE can be realized, but also how it can address contemporary educational inequities and revitalize public schooling in the United States.

CHAPTER 2

Unpacking Human Rights Education

A Framework for Centering Dignity

> [HRE] promotes people learning to safeguard and hold fast to their dignity and freedom—women, men, and children engaged in learning about human rights in the context of their struggles and their daily lives. (Koenig, 1997, p. xii)

Since the enactment of the UN Decade for Human Rights Education (1995–2004), references to HRE have been increasingly present in global and national educational policies and documents. Not only do international bodies like UNESCO (United Nations Educational, Scientific, and Cultural Organization), UNICEF (United Nations Children's Fund), and OHCHR (Office of the High Commissioner for Human Rights) reference HRE in their respective educational literature, but also many ministries of education explicitly employ an HRE framework when laying out their national educational goals and plans. Loosely defined as a means to both promote human rights and address larger and localized societal concerns and issues (see Andreopoulos & Claude, 1997), HRE remains prominent in these agendas, regardless of whether it is wholly implemented. Using the Universal Declaration of Human Rights (UDHR) as a framework, ministries of education tend to approach the enactment of HRE through methods, beliefs, and programs tailored to their specific national or regional contexts.

The United States, however, is one of the few national entities that does not refer to human rights or human rights education in any official educational policy literature, despite being one of the signatories of the UDHR. While some localized grassroots organizations and nonprofits refer to human rights and an HRE approach,[1] the discourse of human rights is generally absent from educational reform agendas on the local, state, and national levels. Although educational mandates historically have been relegated to state and localized governmental bodies in the United States, the proliferation of federal policies regarding education tends to focus on issues of standards-based reform accountability, choice, and innovation. While there is occasional allusion to democracy (particularly in a section of the No Child Left Behind Act), there is no mention of human rights in any major federal- or state-level educational policy documents. With the increased role of the federal government in education, it seems that an opportunity to press for an HRE rather than a market-based approach to reform has been missed.

This chapter briefly reviews the history and emergence of human rights education globally, and argues for ways that HRE can and should be considered in the United States. In particular, I unpack approaches to and definitions of HRE, particularly in light of its proliferation in educational policies and documents since the enactment of the UN Decade for Human Rights Education (1995–2004). While there are many approaches to HRE that reflect both national and localized goals, I argue that HRE in schools has much potential to transform not just schools, but schooling itself, and consequently to transform the lives of the various actors in those institutions. I contend that if HRE is grounded in concepts of agency and transformation, it is inherently centered on creating a culture of dignity for and among students and teachers. On this basis, I theoretically link HRE to scholarship on democratic education, critical pedagogy, and peace education, to collectively yield a comprehensive form of HRE appropriate for the challenges and opportunities of urban schooling in the United States. While HRE has not been promoted often in the United States, I highlight scholars who are making connections between human rights and other American educational traditions, including social justice and critical multicultural education.

Building off global, national, and localized frameworks developed by practitioners and activists, I thus illuminate the possibilities and necessities of enacting HRE in not just urban public schools, but public schools in general. I assert that HRE can motivate young people to stay in and do well in school, and thus should be seen as integral to reform initiatives that aim to address the opportunity gaps and educational debts (see Ladson-Billings, 2006) outlined in Chapter 1. Since a comprehensive human rights approach to education engages young people as actors in their own learning, and this participatory approach encourages school retention and overall academic achievement, HRE is a vital and organic component of urban school reform.

DEFINING HUMAN RIGHTS EDUCATION

While elements of human rights education have existed in multiple locations and contexts worldwide, its aforementioned proliferation in global and national policy documents reflects how human rights discourse was legitimized through UN endorsements. Beginning in 1948 with the UN adoption of the UDHR, which identified education as a human right and as a pathway to full "human development" and "fundamental freedoms" (see also Andreopoulos & Claude, 1997; Claude, 2011), HRE became prominent in international discussions about peace-building and education, eventually seeping into national mandates (see Bajaj, 2011, 2012; Baxi, 1997;

Zembylas, 2011).[2] These national policies often are framed by UN norma-tive approaches to HRE that, in general, view HRE as both an end goal and a process toward building a universal culture of human rights (Bajaj, 2012; United Nations, 2012). The key concepts and themes that emerge from and drive these documents are notions of equality, dignity, nondiscrimination, peace-building, and people-centered social action and change (see United Nations, 2012). While member state adoption and subsequent implementa-tion of HRE have remained uneven, there is still a general consensus among scholars that these guidelines promote a form of education that serves to inculcate an awareness of and responsibility toward upholding a broader human rights culture. Studies also show the importance of operationalizing approaches to HRE in schools, as means to both instill human rights learn-ing and generate a tolerant and welcoming culture in schools (see APSIDES, 2011; Bajaj, 2012; Kati & Gjedia, 2003; Ramirez, Suarez, & Meyer, 2006; Tibbits, 2008).

Many scholars critique the idea of human rights altogether, claiming that the concept originates from Western visions and ultimately fosters Western cultural imperialism, American exceptionalism, patriarchy, and hegemony (Burke, 2006; Glendon, 2001; Howard, 1997/98; Ishay, 2004; MacKinnon, 1993). Further, many theorists rightly point out that human rights discourses often circulate and operate as tools of oppression, domi-nation, and subjugation, doing more harm than good from the perspective of marginalized populations (Abu-Lughod, 2010; Mamdani, 2009; Massad, 2002). While these critiques reflect much truth, the debates surrounding human rights complicate what often is superficially situated as a polarizing binary in favor of or against human rights. Sen (1999) and Knight (2005), for instance, are among the scholars who point out that conceptions and cultures of human rights often originate from non-Western sources and predate Christianity. They argue that the myriad geneses of ideas of hu-man rights must be unmasked, recovered, and decoupled from Eurocentric thought, and recognized as indigenous to other traditions. Significant schol-arship shows that, at times, human rights discourse has been instrumental in challenging, rather than maintaining, imperial and hegemonic forces (Baxi, 1997; Burke, 2006; Grant & Gibson, 2013). Indeed, some of the strongest supporters of and contributors to the UNDHR and other related documents were from non-Western regions (Glendon, 2001; Grant & Gibson, 2013; Ishay, 2004; Mower, 1979).

As Baxi (1997) suggests, one cannot view human rights, particularly as "produced" and promoted by the United Nations, in isolation from the perspectives and struggles of localized populations outside of this mode of production. He states:

> The single most critical source of human rights is the consciousness of the peo-ples of the world, which have waged persistent struggles for decolonization and self-determination, against racial discrimination, gender-based aggression and

discrimination, denial of access to basic minimum needs, environmental degra-
dation and destruction, and systemic "benign neglect" of the disarticulated, disadvantaged, and dispossessed (including the indigenous peoples of the earth).
Thus, human rights cultures have long been in the making by the praxis of
victims of violations, regardless of how rights are formulated, that is, regardless
of the mode of production of human rights standards and instruments. (p. 142)

As a result, approaches to HRE, particularly when promoted by UN-
based human rights initiatives, require serious engagement with the histories of grassroots human rights movements, with particular awareness of
"a history of everyday moral heroism of diverse peoples asserting the most
basic of all rights: the right to be human and remain human" (Baxi, 1997,
pp. 142–143). In many ways, this speaks to the underlying and generative
principle that defines the enactment and purpose of human rights education:
human dignity. According to Reardon (1996), human dignity is the principle that inherently links the numerous forms of rights and entitlements
described in human rights documents and enacted in ways that vary contextually across the globe. Indeed, human dignity is always mentioned and referenced in UN-related documents about human rights and HRE. I highlight
here, and build upon further in the chapter, human dignity as a concept that
fundamentally—and essentially—drives the localized and context-specific
initiatives and calls for broader forms of human rights education.

Models of Human Rights Education

While the ways in which HRE takes shape, both in orientation and process,
differ in particular contexts, several practitioners and scholars have mapped
the various forms and varieties of HRE. Tibbits (2002), for instance, dif-
ferentiates three distinct educational approaches that aim to support social
change and human development, and, ultimately, help build communities
and cultures of human rights in distinct ways. The *values and awareness
model*, which serves to "transmit basic knowledge of human rights issues
and to foster its integration into public values," generally uses curricula (in
schools and out of schools), public service announcements, and creative outlets as a means to generate interest, awareness, and critical consciousness of
human rights issues (Tibbits, 2002, p. 163). Pedagogical methods can vary
with this approach because it emphasizes specific knowledge outcomes, so
the values and awareness model actually can be incorporated into banking
methods of education, where the teacher simply imparts knowledge and
content on the student, rather than participatory or problem-posing methods, in which students and teachers create knowledge and meaning together
(Freire, 1972/2003).

The *accountability model* is an approach used to train professionals
directly involved in the protection of individual or group rights (police

officers, lawyers, military, journalists, etc.) to either uphold or advocate more effectively for these rights. The main objective of this model is to establish professional responsibility to constituents, and as a result it is rarely employed in schools (unless its purpose is specifically to train teachers and counselors in upholding human rights in their roles and capacities).

The *transformational model* departs from the other two models by centering HRE programming that "is geared towards empowering the individual to both recognize human rights abuses and to commit to their prevention" (Tibbits, 2002, p. 164). This approach has both a collective and an individual focus, often assuming that the learner has direct personal and/or group experiences with human rights abuses. Because this approach locates and views the "learners" as change agents and key actors in bringing about a transformative human rights culture, participatory methods are integral to this mode of education.

Bajaj (2012) and Claude (2011) further tease out the transformative possibilities of HRE when they distinguish between top-down and bottom-up approaches. As an example, UN-produced documents are almost always disseminated from the top down; member states gain favor if they adopt HRE into their national mandates (Bajaj, 2012; Flowers, 2000). While such top-down approaches certainly promote, with varying degrees of success, the expansion of strategies that educate people about human rights, many criticize the potential of top-down approaches because state interests often run counter to upholding rights. The form of HRE being implemented may ultimately lose its transformative and revolutionary edge due to state imposition (Bajaj, 2012; Cardenas, 2005). Bottom-up approaches, on the other hand, engender more possibility for transformation because they are driven by localized social movements that "utilize human rights discourse as a strategy to frame the demands of diverse and typically marginalized social groups" (Bajaj, 2012, p. 18).

Centering Dignity: Transformative Practices and Holistic HRE

Although transformative forms of HRE rarely happen in schools (see Tibbits, 2002), I believe that the transformational model is the form of HRE that is most ripe for radical possibilities in the sphere of schooling. Notwithstanding that this form of education usually happens in social movements or informal educational contexts, schools also can be sites where transformative approaches to HRE privilege the agency, experiences, struggles, and beliefs of "learners," both collectively and individually. Because they valorize learners as agentive actors in their own and their communities' social worlds, these approaches place primacy on human dignity. While these approaches generally are found in grassroots and collective social movements, they also can be enacted in schooling contexts if there is a more radicalized re-conception about the purposes of schooling, one that moves beyond narrow views of academic achievement and toward a holistic endeavor that aims to consider what living in a more humane and just world would be. As noted by Tibbits (2008), human rights education historically "has primarily focused on teaching and learning," and should "eventually [be] seen as part of an overall 'human rights based approach' to schooling, which calls attention to overall school culture, policies, and practices related to human rights value" (pp. 104–106). When HRE moves beyond an emphasis on content and academic learning about human rights, there is much potential in viewing schools as sites of transformation and social change for the students who attend them. Particularly when HRE is attentive to the localized experiences and knowledge of students, as well as participatory processes, skills, and structures that may engage them in social action and change, schools become not only sites for a more holistic form of human rights education, but also sites in which the humanity and dignity of school actors are honored, valorized, and given primacy over dehumanizing approaches that exist in schools.

When schools adopt this comprehensive view of human rights education, they potentially are transformed as sites that build more vibrant cultures of human rights and pursue meaningful societal change. Thus, the implementation of this form of HRE necessarily embraces dialogical, problem-posing, and participatory/praxis methods; multiple, varied, and alternative viewpoints and content; and flattened organizational structures that foster collaboration and connection rather than hierarchy and compartmentalization. If enacted in such a manner, HRE naturally intersects with several subfields, including critical peace education, critical pedagogy, and democratic education, as well as anti-oppressive and social justice education and critical multiculturalism, which have a more recognizable (although still marginalized) presence in the United States.

Bridging Multiple Fields: Critical Peace Education, Critical Pedagogy, Democratic Practices, and HRE

By creating an overall school culture that engages students as transformative agents, HRE is possible and inherently linked to pedagogical traditions rooted in critical peace education, critical pedagogy, and democratic education. Although peace education often is viewed as a field that lacks concrete definition (Bar-Tal, 2002; Danesh, 2006), most scholars agree that it embodies some central tenets of theory and practice that ground the field. In particular, peace education provides the requisite skills and knowledge to move toward an idealized state of peace (Bajaj, 2008; Harris, 2008; Reardon, 1988), one in which positive and negative peace exists, and direct and structural violence is absent (Harris & Morrison, 2003; Reardon, 2001). The recent call for "critical" peace education expands upon existing theories not only by emphasizing the centrality of critical pedagogy (Bajaj & Brantmeier, 2011; Diaz-Soto, 2005), but also by privileging "research aimed towards local understandings of how participants can cultivate a sense of transformative agency" (Bajaj, 2008, p. 135).

Critical pedagogy and democratic processes are at the heart of enacting critical peace education. Grounded in concepts of liberation and transformation, critical pedagogy engages teachers and students in the processes of recognizing and using their own experiences and knowledge as catalysts to transform their lives and social worlds (Freire, 1972/2003). Coined "critical consciousness," these processes call for a dialogical pedagogy among students and teachers and require that educational sites be inclusive, participatory, and democratic. While the concept of democracy, in particular, often is met with skepticism because it increasingly is seen as a closed system that does not respond to people's basic needs (McGinn, 1996), educators can respond to this problem by satisfying a "hunger for real democratization" (p. 342). Democratic education, therefore, needs to be something that is experienced and lived, moving beyond the "engineering of consent toward predetermined decisions [to a] . . . genuine attempt to honor the right of people to participate in making decisions that affect their lives" (Apple & Beane, 2007, p. 9). If schools endeavor to be sites in which *teachers, students, parents,* and *communities* contribute to knowledge construction and decisionmaking, the fundamentals of authentic participation in a democracy can be both learned and practiced. In this way, democracy can be seen more as a "dynamic, striving and collective movement than a static order of stationary status quo" (West, 2004, p. 68).

It is this form of critical peace education, which draws from the traditions of critical pedagogy and democratic education, that most intersects with the holistic form of HRE described earlier (see also Metijies, 1997). Since this human rights approach to education engages young people as actors in their own learning, attention to *process* (re)socializes students academically and is therefore equally as important as the *product* of learning and inculcating human rights values. Reardon (1996) and Zembylas (2011) map possibilities in connecting the two fields, specifically by re-theorizing certain taken-for-granted conceptualizations and practices that ground the fields. Reardon argues that the two forms of education are inseparable, particularly when all forms of violence (which are at the core of peace education) are seen as an assault on human dignity (which is at the core of HRE). Zembylas sees compatibility when human rights themselves are understood as ethical projects anchored in responsibility and empathy. This rests in re-conceptualizing human rights in direct relation to human suffering (rather than viewing them as context-specific entitlements or violations) and by encouraging praxis that ethically responds to that suffering. Zembylas (2011) points out that, in turn:

> This pedagogical praxis does not simply affirm rights uncritically; instead, it
> engages in a serious political analysis that recognizes the dilemmas and tensions
> involved, especially in post-conflict societies. Secondly, this pedagogy does not

only focus on human rights violations but also unveils possibilities for solidarity and acknowledgement of common suffering with the other, as well as the emotions of humiliation and powerlessness that often accompany the reception of trauma narratives. (p. 576)

The emphasis on human suffering need not be applied solely in what are seen as conflict or post-conflict societies, as one could argue that the legacies, histories, and contemporary realities of racism and violence that define and pervade the United States may warrant a similar reconceptualization. Even within schools, students endure humiliating policies that have denied them their dignity, as explained in Chapter 1 and theorized in the work of Tuck (2012). As Koenig (1997) states:

> Humiliation is the enemy of human dignity. Humiliation is a powerful experience, the impasse to being human. In defending our dignity, we refuse to be humiliated. We must recognize this in others. Unless we learn to live a life in which we do not degrade, disgrace, demean, or violate the dignity of the other on any level, personal or communal, the cycle of violence, oppression, and abuse will go on ad infinitum. (p. xiv)

Yet, like human suffering, human dignity—which has remained elusive in the experience of marginalized youth in the United States—can frame a conceptual and praxis-oriented approach to educational policy.

FRAMING HRE IN U.S. PUBLIC SCHOOLS: INTERSECTIONS WITH SOCIAL JUSTICE AND CRITICAL MULTICULTURALISM

Human rights education is not simply left out of policy discourses and mainstream practices in U.S. educational reform; HRE also is decoupled from larger radicalized educational traditions in the United States, including social justice education and critical multiculturalism. Although some scholars and activists have shown how these traditions are intertwined (see Banks, 2009; Grant & Gibson, 2013; Hantzopoulos, 2011b, 2012a), most literature does not make explicit connections between civil rights/social justice struggles and larger human rights movements. The work of the National Center for Human Rights Education, which is an offshoot of the People's Movement for Human Rights Learning, explicitly seeks to make those bridges, because "[U.S.] society, most especially the activist community, have not used the vast knowledge of human rights to its full advantage" (PDHRE, 2014). By viewing connections across multiple U.S. social movements (the civil rights movement, the youth movement, the women's movement, the LGBTQIA movement, the labor movement, the environmental movement, the racial and indigenous justice movement, etc.), the National Center for Human Rights Education endeavors to educate grassroots activists in the United States about how they can and should connect local struggles to a larger global struggle for economic, social, and cultural human rights.

While these intersections and strategies refer to movements, several scholars in the traditions of social justice and multicultural education have now begun to link human rights frameworks to formalized educational practice. For instance, Kumashiro (2008) sees potential in applying a flexible and comprehensive human rights framework to contemporary U.S. education to counter dominant discourses (and resulting degrading practices) and to re-commit to the public good. In particular, Kumashiro urges that the "Left" needs to reframe the dominant (and ideologically conservative) discourses that posit market-based strategies as "commonsense" through a lens of multiple human rights that "encompasses various other rights, framed by the expectation that every human being has worth and value and dignity, not only in the ways that we are similar but also, and perhaps more important, in the ways that we are different" (p. 97). He asserts that this reframing must recognize the interconnectedness of educational rights with broader political, economic, cultural, sexual, civil, social, and environmental rights. By bringing together the multiple struggles for particular rights, Kumashiro envisions the development of a cogent front to pressure for a reversal of current educational trends framed around market-based ideologies.

Similarly, Grant and Gibson (2013) see potential in employing a human rights lens to education in the United States as a means to forge connections among localized inequities, global imperialism, and neoliberal, dehumanizing educational reforms. Theoretically connecting the "global" tradition of human rights education and the "local" U.S. tradition of social justice education, Grant and Gibson argue that both are inherently linked, as they "share commitments and pedagogies that challenge systemic inequalities, promote democratic competence, and advocate for education as a tool of human empowerment and social change" (p. 95). The authors argue that—beyond helping achieve social justice for marginalized communities—coupling these traditions might effectively challenge the neoliberal strategies that inherently undermine the potential of those communities and reframe education as a public good. Rather than leaving human rights out of social justice conversations, educators need to re-couple these "siblings" to truly move toward a more socially just world.

Finally, Banks (2009) points out the relationship among human rights, multicultural societies, and citizenship education in pluralistic nations. He sees potential for using the UDHR as a means toward social justice (within the United States but potentially elsewhere as well), but only if students have opportunities to experience human rights for themselves. He threads together the visions of multicultural education and democratic schooling with human rights by stating:

For human rights ideals to be implemented in schools and to become meaningful for children and youth, these ideals must speak to and address their own experience, personal identities, hopes, struggles, dreams and possibilities. In other
words, for students to internalize the concept of human rights, they must have
experiences in the school, as well as in the larger society, that validate them as
human beings, affirm their ethnic, cultural, racial, and linguistic identities, and
empower them as citizens in the school and the larger society. (p. 101)

Arguing against assimilationist and liberal notions of civic identity and
citizenship education, Banks argues for a form of education that simultaneously honors and validates students' home communities and identities, and
allows them to develop more cosmopolitan identities that transcend (without abdicating) their own. He believes that this inherently promotes human
rights, and thereby will deepen students' understandings of those rights.

HRE IN PRACTICE: GUIDELINES FOR SCHOOLS

It is not surprising that in response to the to over-policing, over-testing, and
generally undignified policies that proliferate in most public schools, youth
and educational advocates in the United States are beginning to urge policymakers and schools to adopt a human rights framework to education. For
instance, the National Economic and Social Rights Initiative (NESRI), after
issuing a report that documents the demoralized and degrading environments that youth in Los Angeles and New York City are subject to, urges for
a form of HRE that "includes not only teaching essential academic knowledge and skills, but also creating a positive school environment, supporting
the emotional and behavioral development of young people, and encouraging students to participate in developing the school policies that impact their
education" (Sullivan, 2007, p. 45). The form of HRE that NESRI prescribes
extends beyond what is learned and taught in the classroom; NESRI envisions HRE enacted in a comprehensive and transformative manner.

Globally, Amnesty International (2012) has urged school actors to in-
corporamate a holistic approach to HRE so that students will assimilate a
culture of human rights in which "all members of a given community understand, value and protect human rights, where the values of equality, dignity,
respect, non-discrimination and participation anchor policies and processes
within the community." To this end, Amnesty International has generated
guidelines and resources to support school practitioners, policymakers, and
activists in creating and becoming "human rights friendly schools."

Amnesty International offers snapshots into schools around the world
that engage the principles outlined in Figure 2.1. At present, schools span-
ning 21 countries are in the network; these schools are moving toward and
have elements of "human rights"–friendly qualities. However, no schools in

Figure 2.1. Amnesty International Principles

10 GLOBAL PRINCIPLES FOR HUMAN RIGHTS FOR SCHOOLS

Non-Discrimination and Inclusion

- A community where equality, non-discrimination, dignity, and respect underpin all aspects of school life
- Provides a learning environment where all human rights are respected, protected, and promoted
- Embraces inclusion in all aspects of school life

Participation

- Encourages all members of the school community to participate freely, actively and meaningfully in school life, including shaping school policies and practices
- Ensures that everyone in the school community has the information and resources they need to participate in school life

Accountability

- Is fair, accountable and transparent in all of its planning, processes, policies, and practices
- Protects all members of the school community by making safety and security a shared priority and responsibility

Empowerment Through Learning and Teaching

- Integrates human rights into all aspects of teaching and the curriculum
- Works to empower all students to reach their full potential through education, in particular those students who are marginalized due to their gender, status, or difference
- Empowers students and staff to become active members of a global community, sharing knowledge, understanding and learning with others and taking action to create a world where human rights are respected, protected and promoted

Source: Amnesty International, n.d.

the United States are featured in and/or part of this network. This omission certainly reflects the extent to which human rights discourse has been specifically decoupled from transformative U.S. schooling traditions, and also tacitly suggests American exceptionalism with regard to human rights. In other words, failure to acknowledge that human rights education also can transform U.S. school culture implies not only a false assumption that the U.S. context is free from direct and structural violence, both within schools and in society, but also that the United States is not engaged in human rights abuses domestically and worldwide, which is untrue.

Figure 2.2. ICOPE's Vision of a Human Rights–Based Education System

A Human Rights based system of public education envisions education as a caring relationship between a teacher, a student and his/her family promoting the full development of each and every child.

A Human Rights based system builds on the knowledge of, and respect for, each student's family, community, language and culture. Schools are the centers of their communities. Parents and their communities are essential resources for the schools, and the community and the city are an extension of the classroom.

In a Human Rights based system, students learn to be citizens by making democratic decisions about their school and community life. The city administration, knowing that schools can't solve social problems by themselves, works to eliminate the poverty and conditions that lead to feelings of hopelessness that affect many of our communities.

Every child has the human right to a quality education in a physically and emotionally safe school environment that fully develops his or her unique potential.

In a Human Rights based education system, there is an equitable distribution of resources without regard to economic status, race, gender or nationality.

The dignity of the child, his or her family and their educators are central to a Human Rights based education system.

Parents, students, educators and communities have the right to participate in decision making about policies and practices affecting their schools and school system. They have the right to information and transparency, the right to monitor the education system and the right to timely and effective remedies when rights are violated.

The checks and balances must include: an independent research organization to study and evaluate the movement towards the Human Rights goals of education; independent financial audits to provide user-friendly, transparent information and to promote accountability for the use of public funds; an independent education ombudsperson to resolve conflicts and provide remedies when rights are violated; and full deliberative democracy in the education system.

City, State and Federal elected officials must foster policies that will eliminate poverty ensuring that every family regardless of race, language or zip code have their basic human needs met.

Source: Independent Commission on Public Education, 2012.

Like the collective at the Dignity in Schools campaign, of which NESRI is a part, the activists who form the Independent Commission on Public Education in New York City (ICOPE) see possibility in applying a holistic HRE model in the United States, particularly as an antidote to current policies. In 2012 they produced a report examining the dominant structures that governed urban schools during Mayor Michael Bloomberg's 12-year tenure. Entitled *Getting out from Under: A Human Rights Alternative to the Corporate Model of Public Education in New York City*, their report was an indictment of the business model of public education and mayoral control.

Instead, they suggest a *human rights model of education* as an alternative to overcome the effects of these market-based public educational reforms and particularly advocate for an approach that gives primacy to democratic processes (including parental and community involvement) and the whole child. Their major goals are to ultimately create a model that "will positively contribute to building a public school system on a human rights framework [that] would not only re-energize the promise of public education but also help the city realize its best self as a democratic, equitable, secure and culturally vibrant place to live" (ICOPE, 2012). Figure 2.2 presents ICOPE's broad vision of a human rights–based system that takes into account many of the qualities of a holistic and multifaceted approach.

CONCLUSION

This chapter has charted the global trajectories and key components of a holistic form of HRE to consider how this approach might transpire in urban public schools in the United States. Specifically, I argue that HRE not only emphasizes content and academic learning about human rights, but is also an approach attentive to participatory processes, skills, social action, and an overall school culture that engages students as active change agents in school. Grounded in concepts of agency and transformation, I showed that HRE is ultimately centered on participating in and creating a humanized culture of dignity for and among students and teachers. This form of HRE builds off several transnational and U.S.-based educational traditions, as well as local, national, and global frameworks for schools, to engender ways HRE is understood as a vital component of urban educational reform. While scholars like Bajaj (2011), Flowers (2004), Reardon (1996), and Tibbits (2002, 2008) demonstrate how HRE can foster attitudes of tolerance, respect, and solidarity within and beyond the school community, as well as increase student social and political engagement, I further contend that HRE ultimately can contribute to school retention and overall academic achievement, particularly when human dignity and the participatory approaches inherent to this concept undergird the enactment of human rights education.

HRE often is referenced, discussed, and even theorized in academic and public literature, yet there is a dearth of examples that educators, practitioners, and scholars can turn to in order to understand how it might operate in practice, particularly under a human rights educational rubric that is specific to the United States. Although ICOPE's (2012) report offers alternatives to the dehumanizing practices that have proliferated under NYC corporate educational reform—suggestions range from rethinking governance, funding, parental involvement, curricular content, and pedagogical practice to discipline—the report contains no examples of schools that already practice some of these prescriptions. While creating guidelines is essential to allow for contextually framed and *sui generis* schools to emerge, illustrative descriptions can provide key insight and inspiration, as well as necessary caution, for those trying to move toward human rights–based practices and hoping to give primacy to the humanity and dignity of students in their school-based practices.

In the remainder of this book, I survey the NYC public school land-scape to draw from existing schools that do in fact use HRE principles in practice, in spite of and in resistance to the dominant policies that undergird contemporary school reform. Although most data and examples are drawn from Humanities Prep, I provide examples from other schools to show how models may differ according to context and to offer empirical evidence of the possibilities of public education at this time. While many of these schools do not explicitly employ an HRE lens, I show that they do place emphasis on cultivating cultures of *care, respect, critical questioning, and participation* to build school environments that ultimately are anchored in human dignity and worth. I thus unite these approaches under and link them to a synthesized human rights rubric. I take up these concepts more explicitly in subsequent chapters to both justify these components and share examples of how they transpire in quotidian school life. By empirically demonstrating how these schools institutionalize pervasive forms of HRE in practice and documenting the struggles and challenges, I show the multiple possibilities that arise when schools create a climate of dignity for those young people who have been denied this education in their schools.

CHAPTER 3

Transforming School Culture by Centering Human Dignity

Infusing HRE in School Reform

While the emphasis on punitive accountability policies had not fully taken root in the early 1990s, many urban school activists at that time had begun to critically question the efficacy of large comprehensive high schools. In particular, there was concern over the lack of support for struggling students, the sense of alienation in a depersonalized environment, increasing issues of safety and violence, and low achievement and high dropout rates for students (Anyon, 1997; Fine, 1991; Hantzopoulos & Tyner-Mullings, 2012; Tyner-Mullings, 2014). Inspired by the type of education that was being sparked by schools like Central Park East and groups like the Coalition of Essential Schools, many parents, educators, and community activists began to found programs and schools that were embedded in democratic structures and principles, personalization, strong student–teacher relationships, project-based assessment, and thematic and culturally relevant curricula (Hantzopoulos & Tyner-Mullings, 2012). It was a unique moment in time to create what became known as "critical small schools" (Hantzopoulos, 2009; Hantzopoulos & Tyner-Mullings, 2012).

Humanities Prep and many of the other schools mentioned in this book are situated in this particular historical context. The original idea for Prep is attributed to one of its founding educators, Harry,[1] although he humbly admits that the contributions of others amplified and helped him realize his vision. Having taught in mainstream schools for 18 years, Harry was noticing more and more students becoming disaffected with their education. He says:

> I guess I intuitively seized the opportunity to create on a larger scale what I'd endeavored to do as a teacher in my own classroom: a humane school environment; an intellectual community; a place of mutually respectful discourse and some significant portion of democracy. Most of what I beheld around me in the larger school contradicted these. The hysterical obsession with school tone; the exclusively law-and-order approach to dealing with kids; the continual derogation of students, generally meaning (though not exclusively) Black and Latino students; the

extraordinary lack of enlightenment in general. I had seen it otherwise, not only in my mind's eye, but in bits and pieces of concrete behaviors at other schools—to a lesser degree—that I'd taught in. I had faith that a more hospitable leadership and structure would move students and teachers in the direction of greater humanity and greater achievement. I don't think my faith has been misplaced. (email communication, January 27, 2007)

Noting that the school culture was becoming increasingly punitive, he began to envision an alternative "hospitable leadership and structure" that would counter this trend. Over the course of a frenzied week, he wrote a behemoth 30-page prospectus on education, placing a copy in the mailbox of every teacher on the faculty.

The revolution Harry hoped to instigate happened gradually, rather than overnight, as only one teacher, Tania, responded to his treatise. Her response reflected similar dissatisfaction with the status quo and spoke to the general disempowerment that she believed most teachers felt. When I asked about why she decided to leave her job as a social studies teacher in the mainstream school, and join what, at the time, seemed like a less secure and unwieldy endeavor, Tania said:

> I worked in the mainstream school for 1 year and I was ready to leave. I didn't realize it was the structure [of the school]. I just felt so, so sad and teachers were—well, the teacher's lounge was just a place to sleep. And the teachers—when you could have a discussion, it was really very much that a few people held court and you were silenced. And talking about teaching was just unheard of. *And I hadn't realized that it was the structure that had beaten them down* [emphasis added]. I just sort of looked at them as unhappy human mass and I don't think I wanted to be a part of it anymore, which is crazy because I felt like it took so long to finish college. It took me 7 years to finish college. And I go and I get lucky enough to come into this school . . . and then, it was just abysmal in terms of the morale of teachers and the sadness. (interview, June 2007)

While Tania's reflection, much like Harry's, at first paints a hackneyed picture of urban schools, both of these educators defy pathologized stereotypes by never blaming the teachers and students who inhabit those spaces. Instead, they suggest that the attributes that permeate school culture are in fact *created and are structural*, and that joy, creativity, engagement, voice, and hope could arise in schools if educators and students were given support and opportunities to create an alternative environment. In Tania's case, her pull to join the new mini-school was driven by this hope to create something different; its vision offered an alternative to the cynicism she experienced at the mainstream school.

Focusing on the stark differences between mainstream urban schools and urban schools that enact aspects of human rights education, this chapter makes the case for placing HRE at the forefront of school reform and anchoring school environments in human dignity and worth. This is increasingly urgent and relevant at a time when educational policies—like those discussed in Chapters 1 and 2—have gone in the opposite direction. Drawing on the experiences of teachers and students in both types of settings, as well as the mission statements of HRE-centric schools, I emphasize the importance of intentionally imbuing care, respect, and participatory processes throughout school culture. While students and teachers generally describe mainstream spaces as demoralizing, alienating, neglectful, and uncaring, they enthusiastically describe HRE-framed schools as inclusive, motivating, caring, and engaging. They describe spaces in which their contributions, ideas, and expertise are honored and matter, in contrast to traditional environments where these elements are devalued or ignored. I conclude that these distinguishing characteristics ultimately contribute to students' academic success, and thus assert that building a culture of *care, respect, critical questioning, and participation* is a model for HRE praxis in schools.

TEACHERS SEEKING ALTERNATIVE MODELS: MAINTAINING TEACHER WELL-BEING

During Prep's years as a half-day mini-school from 1993–1997, it was still under the principal leadership and auspices of the larger mainstream school but was allowed to function somewhat autonomously. Some additional teachers, all of whom were from the mainstream school, joined and taught in the program, which eventually enrolled about 60 students annually. Lawrence, who eventually became principal when Prep became an autonomous school in 1997, was compelled to join the endeavor because of the program's emphasis on democracy, a concept that was explicitly woven into the school's mission statement, along with themes like humanization, personalization, and intellectual engagement. Upon reflection 15 years after the program began, Harry describes the vision and purpose of the school at the time, which extends to the present:

It's to provide kids with a liberating educational experience that's culturally rich and that evolves out of—and this is a somewhat conservative idea—some of the greatest thoughts and the greatest ideas that people have ever had, and that is also personalized so that kids have a specific relationship to their learning. And to provide this kind of education for a whole cross-section of kids who may or may not have in some way or another articulated their disaffection about the kind of overly objectified type of education that they have received, that kind of excludes their own psyches. . . . So there's a social mission and there's an intellectual mission. And the intellectual mission I guess is that knowledge and the pursuit of wisdom are a passion of the mind and therefore you know, to quote Sartre, "I choose the world." Because there's also—I think that it's an anti-intellectual, anti-educational society and it's also a society who has chosen to forget about a lot of people, a lot of kids. And I'm interested in those kids. I'm interested in all human beings and providing everybody with a humanizing experience. . . . So we loved kids, we wanted to talk to kids; we were interested in talking to kids. We didn't see their lives as irrelevant to ours, or our real life as irrelevant to theirs. We saw kids as human beings and often flawed as we all are, so we were willing to talk to them about what they were doing, what they were feeling, and how they were acting. So I think that was very, very effective. I think that continues to be effective . . . I guess another way of putting it is having close personal/professional, but more personal relationship with kids. (interview, June 2007)

In these words in particular, Harry describes his reasons for creating Prep as an institution that was intentionally and deliberately in counter distinction to what was happening in schools and in society at the time. Much like how Freire (1972/2003) viewed possibilities in education, Harry thinks of schools as liberating and as sites for speaking and thinking about one's own social world in relationship to the larger world.

This vision specifically attracted many of Prep's teachers and eventually laid the foundation for the school when it became fully autonomous in 1997.[2] Several describe a conscious intention to seek out an alternative schooling environment that not only allows them to put particular educational ideas into practice, but also frees them from the confining structures that characterized their previous schools. In other words, most teachers at Prep describe actively seeking an environment that challenges and disrupts traditional schooling processes that restrict both students and teachers. As Tuck (2012) points out, the recent market-based and rigid policies not only push students out of schools, but also teachers.

Teachers choose Prep for many reasons, including its emphasis on project-based assessment over standardized testing; in particular, Prep is based on "progressive" educational principles not often found in traditional public schools.[3] Andrea, a math teacher, came to Prep because she was drawn by its affiliation with the Coalition of Essential Schools. At the time, Andrea was looking for teaching opportunities only in schools that were actively against administering Regents exams, because she felt the exams were overemphasized and obscured other necessary educational endeavors. Andrea had worked in another public school for a few years and was disillusioned with teaching in them, particularly with "how kids were treated" (interview, March 2007). Before starting her teaching career, Andrea had worked for a not-for-profit that engaged "street youth"; she felt that the organization's approach was much more in touch with the psychological and emotional development of youth than were mainstream public schools. She wanted to leave the public school where she was teaching because of the "restraints on kids' personalities" and described being more interested in seeing kids through a social, cultural, emotional, and developmental lens rather than solely an academic one.

When she met Prep staff at a job fair, Andrea was elated to discover that the school did not focus on whether kids could wear hats or do-rags; she found the school was more focused on students' engagement and growth than on "controlling their bodies." Upon discovering that the school made decisions through consensus, Andrea remembered how effective this strategy had been at her previous not-for-profit job. Overall, she felt that Prep was committed to respecting students and she felt compelled to apply to and work at Prep.

Adrian describes an analogous experience of feeling confined at his previous teaching job. When I interviewed Adrian, he seemed to describe an atmosphere that did not center the dignity and humanity of the students:

> When I started teaching in New York City I was a Teaching Fellow, which meant I basically had to go where they put me. . . . In many ways I felt like I hadn't really had the opportunity to be in a school where a lot of the educational theories I believed in were actually being tried. I was sort of coping with what I think is very typical in a lot of urban schools, which is the overwhelming concern with school safety, and turning around a "failing" school creates this culture of perpetual anxiety and creates a lot of really unfortunate thinking about kids. So the school I was in had very limited understandings of kids. They got their graduation rates up, they got their Regents pass rates up, but . . . the means by which that was happening was pretty atrocious. . . . So I hadn't had yet as a professional educator an opportunity to be with other professionals who thought what I thought and who were trying the kinds of things that I believed in. (interview, May 2007)

Nonetheless, Adrian knew another way might be possible because of his experience, as a teen, attending a high school that was part of the Coalition of Essential Schools. He continued:

> Seeing that Prep was so interested in engaging teachers and thinking about how the school ought to be run . . . to me—at first anyway—seemed like a dream come true. Certainly since then I've realized that that mode of running a school has its own challenges, but all these things came together to me to say this is a place I need to experience. (interview, May 2007)

Both Adrian and Andrea point to the lack of care, respect, and input they had experienced as teachers in mainstream urban schools, which resulted in harmful assumptions about and policies toward kids. Prior exposure to participatory practices, however, may have contributed to these teachers' desire to be part of a professional learning community in a school setting that allows them to sustain hope and possibility about teaching and youth. Similarly, Nick had interned at Prep and wanted to work in a professional environment not only where he was valued and his input respected by his colleagues, but where a holistic perspective on student development was pervasive:

> I obviously was making a much more active choice to be in a place where I thought that I could bring a social work sensibility and training to an educational setting, and that would be welcome. Because there's the knowledge here that the "personal" and academic overlap . . . so there's a need to have someone like a social worker here. It was also helpful that I'd been a teacher here and I knew the institution, but my goal was to be integrated as much as possible. I think that's actually the reason I got hired is because I most of all wanted to be part of the consensus and part of the teaching staff as much as possible . . . and to bring clinical work into this setting. (interview, March 2007)

Nick's comment about "consensus decisionmaking" is a key feature in the establishment of this professional community because it reinforces other democratic principles many teachers hold dear.

In fact, every staff member I interviewed mentioned the professional learning community's emphasis on participation, intellectual engagement, and general respect for teacher expertise as reasons for teaching at Prep. In a climate where teacher perspective and expertise are devalued and ignored (Milner, 2013), Prep's respect for its teachers and its emphasis on participation reignited for many who would have left the profession their passion for kids and teaching. Other teachers pointed out that these emphases also extended to students at Prep, and mentioned how that contributed to their reasons for working there. For instance, Moira, a social studies teacher, remarked that she felt attention to kids' perspectives was missing in other schools:

> I came to this school by accident. When I was thinking about coming into teaching, because I was on an academic track . . . I decided that what I wanted to do first was try to get my foot back into high school . . . and that I should get a per diem license and go and substitute in a few schools and visit some classrooms. . . . And I remember being really fascinated. I was in Harry's classroom and kind of watched what he did. I went to a town meeting, and I was completely blown away by the

town meeting. I don't think I had ever been in a place where teenagers had the opportunity to talk, and what they had to say—I was excited about it. (interview, March 2007)

When Moira became a permanent teacher a year after she subbed, she stated that she always kept Prep in mind and jumped at the chance to join the staff when she heard of an opening. Moira also mentioned finding student–teacher interactions that took place outside of the classroom compelling, reinforcing the type of vision that Harry describes as "informal intellectual discourse."

Clarissa, the music teacher, describes something similar. Prep Central, the shared student and teacher space, was the first place Clarissa saw when she came to the school. She was struck by the level of intimacy between the students and teachers in the space. She felt that having a space dedicated to less formal student–teacher interactions was in line with Prep's mission, as it fostered intergenerational connections. Clarissa's story also speaks to the nurturing and caring environment that many Prep students feel lured them to this particular school.

While these excerpts do not reveal what initially motivated teachers to choose their career path, they do bring to light the myriad reasons teachers choose to work at Prep: Prep has a vibrant and intellectual learning community among teachers and democratic practices among students and staff, and sincere relationships seem to transpire among students and staff in the school. In a broader climate where teachers have little agency or control over decisionmaking, testing mandates trump teacher knowledge (see Abrams, Pedulla, & Madaus, 2003) and educators feel disrespected by the mandates thrust upon them (Tuck, 2012). In contrast, educators at Prep feel valued, respected, and supported as knowledgeable professionals with the ability to make decisions. Table 3.1 articulates more concretely some of the practices that foster this kind of environment.

Several other schools in NYC have similar processes in place. The James Baldwin School and the Harvest Collegiate School, both started by former Prep teachers, have all of the aforementioned structures in place. Urban Academy, one of the earlier alternative schools located in the Julia Richmond Complex in Manhattan's Upper East Side, was one of the pioneers of teacher-designed thematic classes. Other schools with larger populations, such as the Beacon School, School of the Future, and East Community High School, organize teachers into groups like Institutes or Streams to give teachers opportunities to engage in participatory practice. These kinds of participatory processes are necessary because they allow teachers to share and expand on their expertise, feel part of a community, and fulfill the most important aspects of the missions of these schools.

Table 3.1. Key Practices at Prep That Value, Respect, and Support Teachers

Prep Practice	Description of Practice
Consensus-Based Decisionmaking	During weekly staff meetings, faculty and staff come together to make decisions about school policies. Grounded in debate over ideas and policies, consensus endeavors to hear all perspectives and ensure that all faculty members can live with the decisions.
Teacher-Led Meetings	Teachers rotate chairing the faculty meetings, so everyone is involved and has leadership opportunities.
Teacher-Designed Classes	While all classes are aligned with state standards, teachers (often collaboratively and/or with input from students) have opportunities to design and create their classes thematically.
Codirectorship	This model has an administrator and teacher serve jointly as directors of the school, although technically, under Department of Education auspices, the principal is still in charge of the school. In the earlier years, the teacher codirector was a permanent position. When the codirector retired, the staff decided to switch to a rotating 3-year model.
Critical Friends Groups	Teachers get together to workshop lesson plans, debrief student work, and brainstorm policy in constructive ways.
Distributive Leadership Roles	Rather than hiring administrators, members of faculty assume various roles to distribute the leadership. In addition to granting teachers more decisionmaking power and involvement, this strategy also keeps class sizes lower because more money is spent on those who teach.

STUDENTS SEEKING DIGNITY AND HUMANITY IN SCHOOLS: MAINTAINING STUDENT WELL-BEING

Although students also are drawn to Prep for a variety of reasons, including the pragmatic (e.g., proximity, sibling at school), many students and their parents sought out and/or appreciate the more humanized culture. It was quite typical, for instance, for 9th-graders to say they came to Prep because they and/or their parent(s) wanted a school that was small in size. Students talked about wanting to be known; while they did not explicitly articulate this, their ideas of being known were/are ultimately tied to being treated with dignity and respect. For instance, Joshua describes seeking a small school:

> Well, when I was smaller I was also in, like, a big school . . . I used to get in trouble a lot, or whatever. But once I left my old school . . . [to come] to my new one . . . it was a smaller environment. And I did better there.

I did better in a smaller environment. So, you know, I still was getting [into] a little trouble over there, so I guess me and my mother and my father figured, alright the smaller the school the better you do. And this is a small learning environment where everybody knows each other, so therefore we figured this would be the best choice. We heard about Prep through my guidance counselor . . . so then my mother came and visited the school and she liked it. It was actually . . . it was actually [one of] my top three choices here. [When asked whether he thinks Prep was a good decision] Yes, I do. I'm doing very good here. I'm doing much better than I was at any other school. (interview, March 2007)

Although Joshua cites the small size of Prep as the main reason he came, he also asserts that being known allows him to thrive academically. This was the case for most 9th-graders, whose families often found out about Prep through various social networks (family and guidance).

Transfer students often sought out the school themselves and were far more explicit about why they wanted to attend Prep. Similarly, older students, some of whom had come in as 9th-graders, talked very differently about their reasons for coming to the school. While they may have agreed that their parents had something to do with the decision, older students offered much more analysis and detail. For instance, Magdalena, a senior who came to Prep as a 9th-grader, talked about her experiences in a large middle school:

Since I'm in middle school, I had, like, a bad time there. Like I used to get [into] a lot of fights and a lot of problems and like I just needed to get away from that. . . . So my counselor knew [the social worker at Prep], and told me, "Listen . . . if you really want to improve and, you know, want to get somewhere in life then, you know, we could find a small school for you. I know just the place for you." So she told me about Prep and so then that's why I signed up for it. (interview, March 2007)

Like most of the 9th-graders, Magdalena was definitely interested in a smaller, safer learning environment. She went on to explain how the environment at Prep also helped her grow as a person and learn and achieve academically:

Well . . . here I feel like I get a lot of support and it's not a conventional school. And, like, I learned so much from here like personally and academically. Like, I guess, like, [it's] the best decision I ever made. [When asked to give examples of why] Sure, well, the teachers here are like my family. Like, I really get to learn a lot from here. Like, it's not just from textbooks. I guess we learn things that we're not supposed to learn [laugh]. It's really exciting. (interview, March 2007)

After completing 4 years (she will take an extra semester to graduate), Magdalena was able to articulate some of the themes that seemed to be fundamental to her positive experience, themes I will explore later, including strong student relationships and an inquiry approach to content and pedagogy in classes that treated her as an intellectual. While these were not the exact reasons that Magdalena came to Prep, these aspects of the school culture definitely compelled her to stay and helped her thrive.

Similarly, Vivian cited Prep's small size as a luring factor, as she had always attended small schools and wanted to continue the trend. When asked whether it was a good decision to come, Vivian shared:

> Yeah, I really like Prep, like being here. I mean, like, when I came here, you know, I immediately made friends, you know. It wasn't really hard for me to make friends, you know, or to speak out. I felt really comfortable. . . . I really like how the classes are structured because it's not like, okay, paper after paper after paper after paper. And, you know, we're not all sitting and just hearing the lecture, you know. And the classes, they aren't modeled after the Regents exams. We don't take Regents except for the English one, which I'm really happy about because I'd rather write PBATs [Performance Based Assessment Tasks]. Because then you get to research something that you're really interested in rather than just, you know, writing, you know, on the Regents and stuff. (interview, May 2007)

While she originally was seeking only a small school, she describes finding at Prep a friendly and comfortable environment, and a curriculum that allows her to pursue her own academic interests. Thus, while school size was a fundamental feature, it was not the only feature that made Vivian's experience positive.

Victor, a senior who transferred into the school when he had to leave his previous school, explained to me that his choice was limited to Prep or "suspension school for a year." Nonetheless, he believed:

> It actually became something good for me, because it diversified my view on things, so it opened me up to a whole other light I probably would have not seen at my old school. . . . Like, just the way everything in this school teaches everything from different perspectives. My old school was very closed-minded. It's kind of like a little factory for business. So we had like 40 students in the class, 45 students in the class, and we copied notes, and we took tests every week. It was like—it wasn't really learning anything, I guess. I didn't feel, like, intellectual. So, yeah . . . yeah, now I definitely believe I am. I mean, before, I really didn't, but now, just the way I think about stuff and . . . yeah, just the way I think about stuff, and that comes out in my writing and everything I do,

and just as an artist. Yeah, I definitely consider myself intellectual. . . . I think I look at education differently. I actually had a class, like, for the philosophy of our education and stuff like that, so because of that now I really look at it in a different way. I mean, every class should be small. You should have a personal relationship with your teacher. You should have extra time. You should wanna learn. It shouldn't be, like, a burden on you, like you feel like that. You should wanna be able to diversify yourself. You should wanna be smart. I mean, why wouldn't you wanna be smart? (interview, May 2007)

Although Victor described Prep as the alternative to "suspension school," he was surprised to find a humanizing atmosphere in which he felt respected and intellectually challenged. He claims that he transformed through his experiences at Prep and has a whole new approach to education and the world.

For all of these seniors, what initially brought them to Prep differed from what kept them there. While Magdalena and Vivian talked about how the school's small size attracted them, and Victor simply needed an alternative, what they highlight are the relationships, the types of classes, and the intellectual vibrancy that was cultivated among the students—all of which relate to the culture of care, respect, critical questioning, and participation that the school promotes.

Alumni recalled similar reasons for coming to and staying in the school. All of the alumni that came in as 9th-graders described Prep's small size as a factor, and many students' parents had wanted to avoid sending their kids to the schools for which they were zoned.[4] For instance, Kevin explained that coming to Prep was not his choice, but his mother's choice. He had gone to Catholic schools most of his life and wanted to continue, but his mom could not afford it. Kevin said, "When it came to choosing a public school, my zoned school was [one] which I definitely was not going to" (interview, December 2007). His mom found out about Prep through another applicant and scheduled an interview for Kevin, and he was admitted. When asked why his mom did not want to send him to his zoned school, Kevin explained that she felt that safety and academics were simply not priorities there.

Other former students described similar concerns about the zoned high schools they had been admitted to. These students did not know much about Prep; in most cases someone intervened on their behalf and suggested Prep as an alternative. For instance, Queenia stated:

I think in the 8th grade, not having any older siblings, I had no idea what the high schools were like. So I chose the high school based on the way they were described in the high school book, and I chose all the worst high schools . . . I mean not academically worst, but just not for me. I chose School X, I chose School Y, based on what they looked like in the high school book. They sounded like they had the courses that I wanted to go into. And while they do have them, it's just not what they're known for and I didn't know that. So my guidance counselor said, "Absolutely not." She found Prep for me at the last minute and she said, "It's the perfect school; it's small and I think you'll do really well there." I said okay and I applied. Once I went for the interview and I met Harry and I believe it was Don, and I got to meet them and the questions that they asked . . . and it just seemed like such an interesting school. As soon as I found out I was accepted, I didn't even question it. I just knew that was the school I was going for. (interview, May 2007)

While many students do succeed and thrive in the schools mentioned—despite the continual systemic neglect hoisted upon these schools—notoriously high dropout rates and reported incidents of school violence make many students and parents wary (see Advocates for Children, 2002). The very policies and practices outlined in Chapter 1 that create dehumanized environments contribute to parents and students seeking alternatives.

Some alumni mentioned that Prep was not their first choice until their interview at the school. Deena, who had an individualized educational plan (IEP), did not get into any of her first-choice schools; Prep was her last choice. She explained that she struggled in middle school because of her learning disability, but after interviewing at Prep, she "felt they saw that I had leadership abilities and qualities," which is why she chose to come to the school (interview, December 2006). Deena also stated that she liked the atmosphere when she visited, particularly the "first-name basis" [for teachers] (interview, December 2006). At her graduation, Deena was school salutatorian. Jenkins, a student who expressed not wanting to go to his zoned school, also described changing his mind, after his interview at Prep, about which school he wanted to go to:

There was this book, when I got out of middle school, my mom showed me this book about high schools and she told me to read it—we read it together actually—and I went through a lot of schools. . . . So I wanted a new surrounding and I love being in the city [Manhattan], so I went to X, I thought the academics was great. I went to visit, to see what it was like . . . but I wasn't feeling the vibe with the people. Then there was Y, I missed the appointment and it didn't work out, and then I came to Prep and I was interviewed. . . . When I first walked in there they asked me questions about how I view the world, what expectations I have for myself. And they made me laugh a lot of times, and I just walked around the hallways and I just fell in love with this school. I just thought it was so ill. I was just like, "Oh man this school is dope, so yeah." (interview, March 2007)

Deena and Jenkins highlight the welcoming environment and personal approach that characterize prospective-student interviews at Prep; in these cases those factors were powerful enough to change the minds of these young people in terms of what school they wanted to attend.

All of the alumni I spoke with who had come to Prep as transfer students had slightly different reasons for their choice. Some, like Victor, had been forced to leave their previous schools. Katerina, for example, was asked to leave her old school because of "bad grades and cutting." Marianna's story was a bit different:

> Prep was chosen for me by my social worker. I was coming from a group home and they [the social worker and the person from the high school placement] thought . . . that Prep would be perfect for me. I was disappointed because I couldn't go back to School X for whatever reason. . . . They didn't really tell me [why]. I think there was something to do with some notion that I wasn't able to perform at that standard because of my emotional distress at being in foster care. It was definitely distressful to be in foster care, but it didn't hinder me from performing in school. I broke down in tears and I had to leave the room. The high school placement lady was very upset for me. When I came to Prep, I know what interviews are like so I was like, "Yeah, I really like this school. I really want to come. It will be great." And my social worker advocated for me somehow and it worked and I got in. And it turns out that it was a very good fit for me. (interview, May 2007)

After her experience attending a prestigious specialized public high school that did not support her social and emotional well-being, Marianna eventually found refuge at Prep.

Other transfer students were not asked to leave their old schools; they were simply aware that they needed a different environment. For instance, Sammy had transferred out of a specialized public high school and his friend recommended Prep:

> So, like I said, Petey went here. And I really, I don't know, I wasn't good, I mean, I was smart. Definitely smart but I just couldn't . . . I don't know. Something about school wasn't working out for me, you know. At least, like, the way they had it set up until that point at School X. It's a good school but only if you're into that kind of way. [When asked what that way was] I don't know, more rigid. Well, definitely a lot more rigid, you know. (interview, April 2007)

Like Marianna, Sammy had attended a prestigious public school and found it unresponsive to his needs. Also like Marianna, Sammy did not necessarily frame his previous school as a bad school; he framed it as a school that "wasn't working out" for him.

A few students specifically mentioned that other schools had not been attentive to their learning disabilities. Shawn, who had just been de-certified from the special education system, stated, "This was the place. This place was found through, like, intensive research. So when my family found it I said, 'You know what . . . anything must be better than what I've been through [in the special education system] the last 8 years'" (interview, May 2007). While the number of students with IEPs at Prep (12%) is on par with the number across NYC schools (11%), many students benefit from the inclusion and self-contained support models the school offers. Because Prep personalizes its learning environment and is relatively small, it is not uncommon for young people without IEPs to also get support in the resource room or get help from one of the Information and Communication Technologies (ICT) teachers in an inclusive classroom.

In several cases, alumni made very stark distinctions between their experiences at Prep and their experiences at previous schools. The qualities that emerge from their descriptions distinguish Prep from typical high schools, or at least the high schools these students attended, and capture what makes Prep unique. For instance, Alejo, a 20-year-old alumnus who attended community college in upstate New York, compares the school he previously attended with Prep:

> Unlike Prep, School X is not community oriented, and it is not focused on anything but academics. Additionally, the class sizes are two to three times the size of Prep's, making the teaching significantly less personal . . . Humanities Prep, however, is a community-sensitive school. With one of the highest ratios of diversity I have seen anywhere, I was exposed to many different cultures and lifestyles. Being able to experience the different cultures allowed me to figure out how I fit into society. Additionally, the orientation toward community affairs that the school has, has afforded me the opportunity to participate in community events and volunteer for community organizations . . . which, in turn, helped me shape my voice, and has taught me how to speak up, and voice my opinion in any forum.

Alejo's description highlights some of the major themes that came up in my research, including the commitment to diversity (respect), the cultivation of voice (participation), and emphasis on public service and action (participation), all of which will be dealt with in later chapters. Alejo couched these approaches to schooling as being distinct from the norms at his previous school.

Nelson had greater criticism of his old school, and public schools in general. When asked to describe his previous school, he stated:

Public schools are a mess. Public schools more often lend themselves to creating mindless students who are taught only to memorize facts from state-mandated learning "materials." The teachers don't care, punishment is more important than learning, and the social structure within the schools is based on class and race and often creates lifelong psychological scars. In short, I hated my old school and most of the people within it; I learned nothing there except how to hate, and maybe a few facts about World War II. (survey, March 2007)

Nelson's description evokes some common critiques about public schools not emphasizing critical thinking and creativity because of the overwhelming focus on standardization. More strikingly, however, he points to how his old school reproduced racist and classist social structures in society at large; he also emphasizes that punishment took priority over learning. Nelson had a remarkably different narrative about his experience at Prep:

Attending Prep was like getting to live in a free country after living for many years in a not-so-free country. Prep works on a different model. While still adhering to state standards, Prep somehow—whether through the spirit of the teachers, or from the diversity of the students, or the emphasis on community—manages to teach and inspire within the mess of public education. The difference between Prep and other schools is so obvious to me—because I experienced it—that I have trouble describing it. If not for Prep I would never have gone to college; I would never have been afforded a different point of view; I would have never have enjoyed education; I would never have sought to better myself. (survey, March 2007)

This second passage from Nelson is full of hope and potential. While he seems, at times, unsure about what makes Prep's model unusual, his descriptions actually suggest concrete reasons. Nelson also credits Prep's model for inspiring him to learn and go on to college, among other positive outcomes, although of course there may have been other unmentioned influences and factors. Nonetheless, he suggests that schooling at Prep is unique and reflective of a thoughtful, alternative counterpractice, even as the school adheres to "state standards."

Lisa was so unhappy at her old school that she became utterly disengaged:

I wasn't happy at my old school . . . it's in Brooklyn, also in Park Slope. I was just miserable. It came to the part I was so miserable I was failing. I just didn't care about school. Well, actually it wasn't that I didn't care about school just being there made me lose interest I guess. But I knew that I still, you know, it wasn't me and I knew that the only way to get out of that situation was to change schools. So I made the switch and I called the public schools to see what school would take someone so late. I was at the end of my junior year, that's when I transferred here. So to transfer at that point in high school, you know, it's kind of difficult. So when I called Prep they were the only school that would accept me. (survey, March 2007)

She describes later in her survey a scenario in her old school that indicates that she was failing and on the verge of dropping out:

I left School X because I felt like the primary focus of the school was to mold every one of us into people that they wanted us to be. There was no room for self-expression and individuality. Classroom lessons focused around lecturing. There was no form of interactive learning such as group discussions. There were constant forms of disciplinary actions practiced against petty incidences. Like, for example, the first day of my sophomore year I did not have the money for my books. I did not know that the book money had to be in the first day of class because I did not receive any notice in the mail. Apparently one had been sent out 2 weeks before school started. The book bill was about $80 and my mother told me that she was not going to have the money by the next day, but by next week when she got paid. Because I didn't have the money right when they wanted and refused to acknowledge my financial situation, I was sent to detention. Detention at my school was not a time to do extra assignments or homework like most schools do. We had to stand and face the board until they decided we can go. That day I was there for an hour. It was ridiculous! I was punished for something that was beyond my control. During junior year I was beginning to lose interest in going to school. I stopped going and did not care about my work. This was so out of the norm for me because all my life prior to that moment I was an excellent student. I was failing one class after the other as time passed. I did not want to drop out of school. (survey, March 2007)

Like Nelson, Lisa emphasizes, in more detail, excessive punishment at her previous school. However, she also describes how her experience in school killed her desire to learn, at least in that setting. Her description of Prep is remarkably different:

Transferring to Prep was the best decision I made for myself during my high school career. I saw myself as being more than that [a dropout] and it was at that moment I realized that my future is in my hands. I called several high schools and Prep was the only school that would accept students at any point during their high school career. I was a second-semester junior. I loved Prep! I loved all my classes and I was encouraged to have a voice in the classroom. Prep teachers believed in their students regardless of who they were and where they came from. We were seen as individuals and embraced for it. Classroom lessons were held through group discussions, which helped me retain what I was being taught. I can honestly say that I learned way more at Prep than I did at School X. My education up until Prep seems like one big blur. Prep also made it important that its students would be in touch with the world around them by taking out some time once a week to talk about current events in big group discussions called Quads. Prep opened up my eyes to the world around [me]. Because of Prep I was able to form an idea of what I wanted to do in life. I had realized how much I loved writing and having the opportunity to have a voice, and that's when I thought studying journalism in college was something I was going to do. (survey, March 2007)

In her short description of Prep, Lisa underscores the themes of care, respect, critical questioning, and participation that were pivotal to re-engaging her academically. Lisa experienced these themes through Prep's pedagogy and classes, emphasis on student voice and current events, respect for diversity, and belief in the ability of all students.

CONCLUSION

Overall, the ways students spoke about coming to Prep align with one of the main points of its mission: to provide "a haven for students who have previously experienced school as unresponsive to their needs as individuals." While students' rationales for attending Prep spanned diverse reasons ranging from the school's small size to lack of other options, students repeatedly said that their experience at the school surpassed initial expectations, and that Prep as an institution interrupted some of the alienating processes found in mainstream and traditional schools. A school culture of *care, respect, critical questioning,* and *participation* was embedded in each and every one of these assertions. Student and teacher testimonies demonstrate that structures and policies intended to establish and strengthen these aspects of school culture not only serve to operationalize HRE in schools, but also contribute to greater academic achievement. HRE makes an ethical and material difference in the lives of youth, propels students to engage in democratic citizenship, and combats socioeconomic and educational (structural) disparities by creating conditions that not only promote attendance but also (re)socialize students academically.

Prep is not alone in creating a mission that runs counter to the mission of schools structured in a mainstream way. Throughout this book are examples from other schools in New York City; although they have slightly different foci than Prep, these schools also are committed to participatory, student-centered, and human rights educative practices—the fundamental aspects in building a school environment that is anchored in dignity and human worth. This framing sets the groundwork for the remainder of the book, which emphasizes specific strategies and approaches used by several schools in NYC to enact HRE and these particular aspects of school culture. While many of the schools mentioned do not explicitly call their approaches HRE, their missions and practices emphasize *care, respect, critical questioning,* and *participation*—principles and practices aligned with the aims and goals of HRE. I argue that these foci are not supplemental or secondary to other educational initiatives; instead, they are woven into the fabric of all aspects of curriculum and school life to create fertile ground for learning, especially for those most disenchanted with school. Subsequent chapters will unpack the essential qualities and components for building such schooling environments.

CHAPTER 4

The Components of Care
Ways to Build Transformative Student-Teacher Relationships

> *Giancarlo:* The teachers are great. Like I know Prep hires teachers that . . . have the confidence and the ability to communicate with students . . . down to earth but it's not really down to earth. It's the teachers in Prep understood that they were kids once, too, you know?
>
> *Selma:* They haven't forgotten it.
>
> *Giancarlo:* I don't know. It's just I love Prep. . . . It's not only like the teachers, though. It's also, like you have the cool teachers, but then you also have a cool principal. . . . That makes it . . . the icing on top of the cake.
>
> *Selma:* Not just that, he's so open . . . the thing I like about him was actually when he shares his experience, especially in Quad, when he came and he opened up to us about like his struggle. I loved that, because I felt like, "Wow, this guy like . . . he came a long way." It gives me hope. It gives other students hope, who felt like they've been let down.
>
> *Zack:* . . . he's pretty cool. . . . Yeah, he is coming up to kids in the hallway like, "Yo! . . . That's good. Go to class."
>
> *Selma:* [laughter] Yeah, rather than, "You're failing. Leave." (focus group, May 2007)

This seemingly mundane focus group exchange about teachers between Giancarlo, Selma, and Zack unearths several of the many dimensions of how students conceptualize their student–teacher relationships at Humanities Prep. This small vignette sheds light on what repeatedly came up in my research: Not only are teachers and administrators perceived to be relatable "equals," but ordinary faculty–student interactions at Prep are remarkably different from the "traditional" relationships these individuals experienced in mainstream schools. The tremendously positive descriptions that students offered about most of their teachers at Prep, as well as repeated mention of these teachers even when not prompted, reflect the fact that intergenerational relationships at Prep were pivotal to students' experiences and overall perception of the school. Their dialogue illuminates not only how these students felt about the personal relationships with their teachers, but also how this experience differed completely from their perceptions of and interactions with adults in other schools.

The topic of student–teacher relationships is not particularly new to human rights education, as it is central to the pedagogies and approaches that frame the field (critical pedagogies and, by extension, democratic education and critical peace education). As discussed in Chapter 2, these approaches, influenced by the work of Paolo Freire (1972/2003), assume that the traditional student-teacher relationship is inherently oppressive and hierarchical. This relationship not only perpetuates inequality between student and teacher, but subsequently maintains this dichotomy among "oppressed and oppressor" in society at large. To resolve this tension, critical educators insist that the nature of the relationship must transform through critical dialogue so that power—once located solely in the teacher's hands—can shift to the students, reversing roles so that teachers can validate and affirm the knowledge of students. This approach presumes that sharing knowledge and power in the classroom erodes the typical authoritarian student–teacher binary, liberating the student from the oppressive nature of the relationship (and societal oppression at large), so that transformative learning experiences can begin and seemingly translate into the dismantling of societal inequalities. Although Chapter 8 looks more closely at and grapples with some of the critiques of democratized and critical pedagogies and theories, both in fundamental premise and in practice, this chapter specifically examines the ways that students view more horizontal relationships with their teachers as essential to creating a more dignified and humane learning environment.

In particular, while the transformative relationship is embedded in assumptions about social change, structural inequality, and liberation, it also is embedded in the belief that *caring* relationships between students and teachers will lead to increased success for students in school. Noddings (1992), the scholar frequently associated with this literature, has suggested that schools shift away from competitive models of education to embrace qualities that emphasize nurture, collaboration, and care. She argues that, in turn, schools will become places in which all types of professions, abilities, and people are valued. While many scholars agree that schools need to be caring and nurturing places, some also posit that definitions of caring are laden with cultural assumptions and do not inherently translate easily across specific contexts. For instance, Valenzuela (1999) and Antrop-Gonzalez and De Jesús (2005), in their studies on Latino youth, found that teachers need to be responsive to students' cultural backgrounds, and thus they advocate for "authentic caring" or "critical care" in schools. Bajaj (2009) adds a new dimension to this debate by suggesting that studies of caring have been "context-blind" and calling for greater consideration of the greater social, economic, and political structures that surround schools to comprehend what happens within them. Others, like Bartlett (2005), address the limitations of student–teacher relationships that employ a "friendship-like strategy"; namely, her findings show that these strategies often do little to raise critical consciousness among students, particularly when devoid of a more localized understanding of contexts in which these relationships transpire.

This chapter takes up these issues and illuminates the qualities of care, with specific focus on how strong student–teacher relationships can help build a culture of human dignity and worth for students in public schools. While there is a substantial body of literature that describes the importance of student–teacher relationships in addressing inequities in schooling (see Antrop-Gonzalez, 2011; Bajaj, 2009; Bartlett & García, 2011; Bartlett & Koyama, 2012; De Jesús, 2012; Hantzopoulos, 2011b, 2012a, 2012b; Rivera-McCutchen, 2012; Rodriguez & Conchas, 2008; Tyner-Mullings, 2012), this chapter takes a new approach by placing youth perspectives at the center, advancing student–teacher relationship research by addressing a gap in the literature regarding how students describe and understand these relationships. In particular, I show the specific qualities that youth at Prep ascribe to positive relationships with their teachers, to provide a more complete picture of how HRE lends itself to a culture of care, specifically regarding the role and importance these relationships play in students' academic trajectories. While other practices and structures at Prep that contribute to students' academic (re)socialization will be explored in subsequent chapters, I demonstrate in this chapter how youth view student–faculty relationships as paramount aspects of their schooling experience. Given these findings, macro-educational policies cannot overlook the importance of relationship building as one of several features in reframing school reform, both as a way to transform schools into spaces and experiences more conducive to learning and, by proxy, to increase graduation rates and opportunities for youth.

BUILDING STRONG STUDENT-TEACHER RELATIONSHIPS: THE ELEMENTS OF TRANSFORMATION

As described in the previous chapter, many current and former students at Prep overwhelmingly describe their relationships with teachers and other adults in the school as positive and unlike anything they previously experienced. While some students are vague in their descriptions, simply stating, as Victor did, that "you get a closer relationship with all the students and teachers" (interview, May 2007), most students distinguish particular qualities that make these relationships unique. Themes that emerge from these descriptions include: teachers as equals, a culture of trust, a culture of care, the concept of family, and teachers as friends. Although several of these themes overlap and reinforce one another, I will show that each theme clearly demarcates specific characteristics of positive relationship building between students and teachers.

Teacher as "Equals"

One thematic description consistently used by students to describe their relationships with teachers is egalitarian. For instance, Franz, an alumnus,
writes the following in a survey that asked him to summarize his experience
at Prep: "The teacher/student boundaries were blurred, and the teachers
learned as much from the students as the students did from them" (2007).
Franz suggests that not only do students gain from this relational paradigm
shift, but teachers do as well. In many ways, this statement evokes Freirean
visions (1972/2003) for relationships in which hierarchies are flattened and
knowledge is co-constructed and shared. Similarly, Dalia, another alumna,
describes how student–teacher relationships are more horizontal:

> There was no structure or Apartheid, if I can use that word, between
> teachers [and] students. Everyone interacted with each other, everyone
> looked at one another as equals and it created a true sense of democracy
> within a school, which is quite rare. (survey, 2007)

For Dalia, student–teacher relationships extend beyond equalization
and represent a more vibrantly democratic community. Antonia, another
alumna, also notes the effects of these horizontal relationships on her school
experience:

> Prep became my family when I felt I had no one at home. I feel that my
> teachers were my equal, not so much of an authority figure, which made
> me want to excel and make them proud. (survey, 2007)

For Antonia, the flattened nature of student–teacher relationships not only
contributes to a sense of belonging (by being familial), but also fuels a sense
of academic accountability that is catalyzed by her commitment to her
teachers and her community.

Students suggest that the ability to call teachers by their first names reinforces the idea of reciprocity between students and teachers. While calling
teachers by first names also may be incongruent with deeply cultural beliefs
about how to address authority, many students describe that this practice,
in the particular schooling contexts from which they were coming, enabled
them to feel less alienated by school. Thus, while many students express being at first unaccustomed to this practice, most speak very fondly of it and
acknowledge that it diminishes the traditional hierarchical structures that
pervade most school environments. For example, when Jessie, a senior, is
asked what she likes best about the school, she states:

> I also love Prep for that we don't call our teachers by their last names.
> It's more personal . . . once you call teachers by their last name you feel

like it's an authority figure and you feel like there's a barrier between you and the teacher. That is just somebody who's telling you what to do and when to do it. (focus group, May 2007)

Jessie insinuates that, through this simple act of using first names, the first step toward equalizing the relationship between student and teacher has been taken, regardless of the actual content of the exchange. Luis, a Prep alumnus and student at Hunter College, also points to how this type of exchange resituates the meaning of "student":

Like, they're [other schools] definitely lacking in . . . teacher–student relationships. I thought it was great that I was able to call my teachers by their first name. You know, because it made their relationship more personal and it made it more . . . a one-on-one thing rather than, you know, you're just a student in the class. (interview, March 2007)

Since he is no longer engaging as "just a student in the class," but rather in a "one-on-one thing," Luis suggests that the first-name policy at Prep indeed helps to create a sense of equal status with teachers. Rather than just being a subordinate student to a teacher, he intimates that his humanity and individuality are recognized. Additionally, Luis positions Prep as different from other schools, suggesting that relationships at Prep interrupt the alienating processes between students and teachers that are seemingly intrinsic to traditional schooling, as documented in previous chapters.

Similarly, Pedro, another alumnus who is currently a student at CUNY/John Jay, illustrates:

The teachers there really . . . bring themselves down . . . to the same level as the students where you can talk, like one-on-one with them. Just even the smallest things as, like, calling them by their first name makes it really personal and they're really there for the students. (interview, May 2007)

Like Luis, Pedro describes how the first-name policy made for a more personalized and equalized environment. Yet, he also suggests that this lays the groundwork for creating a supportive environment by stating how "even the smallest thing" makes students feel comfortable enough to talk "one-on-one" with their teachers. It is this type of nurturing environment that helps kids enjoy and want to come to school.

A Culture of Trust Between Students and Teachers

Students often describe their teachers as "trusting" and subsequently indicate that this makes them feel acknowledged as agents and decisionmakers in their own education. For instance, Lulu, a transfer student, distinguishes Prep from her old school when she notes that "the overall difference between Prep and my old school is that I have more freedom to shape my education and responsibility in the choices I make" (survey, 2007). For Epiphany, an incoming 9th-grader, acts of trust manifest in simply being allowed to go out to lunch, something that very few NYC public high school students are permitted to do. While this seems rather mundane and simple, it is a gesture that can inspire confidence in students. As Chakasia, a transfer student previously labeled as "truant," notes:

> Prep has taught me to be more responsible in a way because in my other schools, I never went out to lunch or anything like that, so just me coming back, that tells me a lot about myself, 'cause I could just go home and stuff like that. But I come back, so, in a way, it's made me more responsible and more mature, I would say. (focus group, May 2007)

Students intimate that by having choices and decisionmaking power, they feel more responsible.

Other students describe how teacher trust translates into academic success. For example, Zack, a transfer student from another alternative school with a similar mission and population, distinguishes how teachers trusted student judgment at the two schools:

> I feel like I got out of Prep a bigger sense of responsibility, because you have to choose your own classes, and once you choose your classes then you really don't have the right to complain about it, because you chose that. I don't know. I feel like I am prepared to go to college, or into some other higher form of education. Before, when I went to School X . . . well, they call themselves an alternative school but really, there's really not much alternative about it. You . . . basically have your classes that they give you. You stay in the same class with the same people. You go and you learn what you learn, and that's what you learn, and that's it . . . . I like Prep because you just . . . get to choose your classes . . . the things you want to learn, and I think that's cool. (focus group, May 2007)

Thus, the level of curricular choice (within the parameters of state guidelines) engenders not only a sense of responsibility and maturity in the students, but also a feeling of being trusted by their teachers. In turn, the emphasis on student decisionmaking contributes to successful academic re-engagement of students, as they feel responsible for the actions and choices they are making in their education and broader lives. While seemingly mundane and simple, trusting students to make choices where traditionally they have had little agency honors their dignity by promoting a form of self-determination.

A Culture of Critical Care

Students also describe explicitly their relationships with teachers as being embedded with care and, in particular, the previously defined concept of "critical care" (see De Jesús, 2012). Studies by De Jesús (2012); García, Flores, and Woodley (2012); Rodriguez and Conchas (2008); and Valenzuela (1999) show how caring relationships between teachers and students that are constructed in specific contexts translate into increased student engagement and academic success, particularly for Latino students who historically have been and contemporarily are underserved by public and Anglo-dominated educational institutions. This study is not specifically about Latino students, nor is it about a Latino-centric community–based school. Nevertheless, Prep students—many of whom previously felt alienated from schooling for any number of reasons—describe several characteristics of care that echo some of the ways caring operates within a more critical framework that seeks to redress inequities in schooling.

One common way that critical caring transpires at Prep is when teachers go beyond their pedagogical duties to check in with students. Reneka, an alumna attending college, remembers her experience:

> I mean the counselor that I went to . . . helped me when I was having problems in the house [at home with her family]. You know it was just . . . organized so you would be able to talk about stuff that's going on in your house. Teachers were really concerned. (interview, March 2007)

Similarly, Jonathan, a junior who left Prep for a semester and then came back, states:

> I felt that the school was not really my thing. And then I realized that it was . . . a home away from home. And the reason I say that is because the teachers just concern [themselves with] everything around you. Everything that you do is their business and that's a good thing . . . if you do something wrong, they don't look over you for it. And they're just going to make sure it's all right. You know, to make sure that you're doing fine and they check in with you every step of the way to make sure you're doing a-okay. (focus group, May 2007)

The way Jonathan describes *how* teachers cared is evocative of a critical care approach; teachers take interest in students' lives but also hold students accountable for their actions, in supportive ways.

For some students, this type of care and interest translate into higher expectations for themselves. For example, Mattias, a senior, explains in a focus group:

It's given me opportunity, 'cause you know before I came to this school, I wasn't that kind of good kid or whatever . . . I wasn't at all. I was trouble—doomed or whatever. I feel like coming to this school, everybody's so nice to each other, especially if you have the teachers who really care about you, you start to realize, you know, the teachers are going fifty [meeting halfway] with you, so you may as well put the other fifty in to complete the circle. (May 2007)

Mattias describes how teachers' high, yet supportive, expectations of him encourage him to be his best self. Despite describing his previous self as "doomed," Mattias graduated shortly after this research and won a prestigious 4-year leadership scholarship to a competitive liberal arts college. His teachers' heightened expectations ostensibly contributed to a shift in his own perception of himself from "trouble" to "good kid" and capable student. As Serena, a recent transfer student, notes, this care boosts her self-esteem: "I guess the bottom line is that the teachers in Prep . . . they care. I mean, they give you a sense of . . . confidence" (focus group, May 2007).

Some students link the culture of care and increased academic performance. For example, Chakasia relays this in a focus group:

Well, I feel that I got a better education here at Prep, being that the teachers, they help me with everything. If I have a problem, they'll help me with it. They make sure I understand the work that I'm doing, and they're always there to help me with anything, so I like that about Prep, because my other schools weren't like that, unfortunately. (May 2007)

Similarly, Victor, a senior who transferred from another public school because he violated a disciplinary code, describes how critical care ultimately supports learning:

They just care about, like, students and about teaching more than they care about money or doing research papers, anything like that . . . you will get the personal attention that you need here to learn whichever way you need to. So you won't just learn it; you'll actually absorb the information, actually, like, know what you learned. I think that's the big difference between here and other schools. Other schools, you'll learn something, and you'll remember it, but you really, really won't know what it means. But here, you will. (focus group, May 2007)

Through his description of how teachers care, Victor explains how personal relationships translate into a pedagogy that enables students to encode materials more effectively. Like other students, he uses teachers at Prep as a barometer by which to measure teachers in other schools, reinforcing the notion that in students' eyes, previous schooling had been unresponsive to their emotional *and* academic needs.

In addition, Prep students and alumni explain that high expectations make them feel validated as contributors to knowledge production. For example, Epiphany describes her transition from middle school to high school when talking about Prep teachers:

> The teachers here . . . they're very understanding . . . my old teachers, if you said something to them that they didn't like, they would give you a detention, an in-house or whatever. But this school . . . you can say, "Oh, I think this was a boring subject," and they [the teachers] can be like, "Well, how can we make it better?" They actually ask you, "How can we make it better?" They actually listen to your side. They actually want to know how you want to be teached [sic]. You can say, "I learn better if we watch a movie. I learn better if we read from papers. I learn better if we just talk. I learn better if we work in groups." They actually try to make it that so everyone learns comfortably. (interview, March 2007)

Thus, the view that teachers are more understanding and more pedagogically responsive to student needs fuels an overall sense of academic pride and success. For students like Ray, a 12th-grader, this level of student attentiveness and personalization allows teachers to better understand his capabilities:

> All the teachers are really committed towards helping you achieve whatever your goal is and I think it's really helpful that they challenge and push you a lot . . . [like] Tania in Global. I feel like I'm doing a lot of work for her class . . . but even though I'm doing more than she's doing with the assignments, she still sees room for improvement. Even though I've already met her standards when she gave the assignment, she still says, "Well, in terms of just writing period, there's things that you can do to make your writing better, so revise it like this and just start thinking about it like this and just keep working." That kind of pushing and hearing that you're not as great as you think you are all the time really helps you drive yourself and want to achieve more. (interview, March 2007)

In Ray's case, he explains that this attentiveness and subsequent encouragement help him push his thinking and realize his own academic potential in a nonthreatening way. In this sense, caring does not reveal itself just when teachers are uncritical of students, but caring manifests when high expectations are maintained for students in a supportive educational environment; this is suggestive of the notions of critical care (Antrop-Gonzalez & De Jesús, 2005).

Teachers as "Family"

Use of the word *family* and familial descriptors (e.g., second home, parent, sister) came up frequently when students talked about Prep. As Khadija, an alumna, states in her survey, "When I attended this school, I felt like I had a second family in most of the students and teachers" (2007). In many ways, this is an extension of the type of critical care discussed earlier, but it further suggests that many teachers and students at Prep look out for one another as one looks out for someone in her/his own family. For instance, Lisa, an alumna, explains how for her the student–teacher binary dissolves at Prep through the family-like relationships:

> It's hard to find teachers in other high schools that are like Prep because they're very focused on you as an individual, they really want you to excel and it's more of like . . . let me see . . . the relationship, yeah to some extent it is teacher–student, but it's more of a family and they really genuinely care about the students so even if you do have an issue it's not like, you know, you have to worry about being reprimanded or you're going to be punished or sent to detention. It's more of like having that open communication as a student, which is really important. (interview, March 2007)

As mentioned in relation to other data, the level of personalization at Prep contributes to a type of genuine and critical care that is, for Lisa and for others, much like what they expect from family. This resonates with how Valenzuela (1999), in her study of Mexican American youth, conceptualizes how caring relationships might transpire between students and teachers—relationships characterized by students and teachers sharing culturally bound concepts of caring. Rather than applying their own conception of what it means to care, teachers in this new paradigm of care understand and take into consideration what caring might mean to their students, resulting in more alignment between them through this reconceptualization.

Prep students describe a family-like environment of accountability in which their teachers maintain strong disciplinary boundaries and nurture them at the same time, something that many students feel resonates with what a familial caring environment should be. Vivian explains:

> I guess like some of the ways the teachers act towards me is kinda like how my mother and sister act towards me. Like if they know there's something I shouldn't be doing they're like, "You know you shouldn't be doing that," which is something that my sister and mom say. And, you know, if I do a good job they congratulate me and they're really nice to me and they make Prep feel like a second home. (interview, May 2007)

In this case, Vivian describes how Prep teachers dispense advice and show pride in a loving and concerned way that reminds her of relationships of care within her own family. Vivian's tone indicates that her teachers' advice is perceived not as patronizing but as reasonable and sincere. Because teachers at Prep challenge students to think about their decisions and actions, Vivian feels cared for in a more authentic and "critical" way. Joshua, a 9th-grader, explains student–teacher relationships in similar terms:

> It's a big family and we share knowledge with each other. . . . The teachers are—they're like school parents. They're like parents that teach. They push you and they push you and if you don't get the push and you don't get it and act right, then they'll fail you, but they're not going to fail you for nothing . . . they also offer, like, help. Like you don't have to go up to them—you know because a lot of people don't like going up to people asking for help. They offer it to you. (focus group, March 2007)

In some ways, Joshua describes an environment of accountability wherein failure is not an option because the teachers at Prep are like parents who want their children to succeed; they set high expectations but with a lot of encouragement and support. In this sense, students at Prep feel that their teachers care about academic and emotional well-being holistically, as a family member would. This culture of critical care clearly influences the ways in which students engage in school life.

Teachers as "Friends"

Another descriptor Prep students use to talk about their teachers is "friends." In many ways, the characteristics ascribed to teachers as friends are similar to the characteristics of teachers as family. However, one distinction is that friendship has a more symmetrical connotation than "parent" or "older sister." For instance, Vivian, who earlier described teachers as being like family, states that "teachers are also like friends instead of just, you know, people who teach you" (interview, May 2007). Vivian says that when she describes Prep, friends who attend other schools are envious because:

> I tell them, "Oh, I'm actually happy to get up and go to school in the morning," and I tell them that the teachers are really nice and that it's not all work, work, work with them. . . . You know, we can also talk to them just as, you know, we talk to our friends. (interview, May 2007)

Pedro echoes this sentiment. When asked what to keep about the school, he states, "Have the faculty be there for the students. It is really different from other schools. The faculty can really be . . . your teachers and your friends at the same time" (interview, May 2007).

What is interesting about these students' views is their common understanding that strong student–teacher relationships are more than students conversing and being comfortable with teachers; students at Prep feel like an "equal partner" in the conversation. As noted with first-name basis relationships, students at Prep appreciate the equalizing aspects of their relationships with faculty. Describing teachers as friends assumes a degree of symmetry in the dynamics of the relationship. While some students seek advice from their teachers, which may connote a more traditional, hierarchical relationship, students also talk about seeking advice from their friends. The ways that students regularly describe their teachers as friends suggests that there are genuine attempts to engender an intergenerational, authentic dialogue among all school actors at Prep, which reflects the democratizing and humanizing environment the school seeks to cultivate in its mission. Reneka, an alumna currently at Dillard, notes:

> They are not like teachers, they are more like friends. . . . We weren't just any number in Prep—teachers actually knew your name, and when you'd see them in the hallways, they'd have a discussion with you. Not like a regular high school where teachers just walk by you, and they just call your name and take your attendance and that's about it—don't know anything about you. At Prep, they actually talk with you. (interview, March 2007)

When describing her teachers as friends, Reneka does not use the expression talk "to you," but rather "with you," implying a more symmetrically perceived relationship that engenders respect for her as a fellow human being. Despite using descriptors like "teachers," Reneka suggests that these relationships transcend typical student–teacher relationships and contrasts her experience with that of a "regular high school."

Prep students note that this type of rapport also extends regularly into scenarios beyond the school. For example, Victor states, "I like the close relationship with the teachers the most. Because in no other school have I gone to dinner with teachers I had, or lunch, or just talked about my regular life or anything like that. So that's probably to me the best part of Prep" (interview, May 2007). Victor is referring to a common practice among several teachers at the school: They take students to lunch to discuss their academic and personal situations. Reneka, who was quoted earlier, feels that because she had experienced such close relationships with Prep teachers, her college professors—adults in positions of power—seem "more approachable" (interview, March 2007). Sebastien, a current senior, describes a similar situation, by stating that "meeting these teachers . . . I'm able to communicate with adults . . . [in ways] that I have never been able to with any other kind of person before I came to this school" (focus group, May 2007). By helping these young people develop the skills and confidence to approach and interact with adults in general, the student–teacher relationships at Prep do not just help students do well in high school, but also prepare them to interact as equals with their elders in the realms of work, school, and community.

THE CASE FOR BUILDING A CULTURE OF CRITICAL CARE

As suggested by the students' descriptions of their teachers, strong student–teacher relationships are pivotal to the ways that students experience schooling. In the case of Humanities Preparatory Academy, these relationships help cultivate a sense of welcoming and belonging that contributes to students' positive perceptions of and experiences with school. In addition, current and former students describe how strong intergenerational relationships at Prep promote academic and social growth that impacts these young people in numerous positive ways. The central role that student–teacher relationships play in these students' experiences warrants attention, particularly in a broader climate where educational policies are continually framed around notions of "accountability" rather than human dignity. The characteristics students ascribe to these relationships—teachers as "equals," as "trustworthy," as "caring," as "familial," and as "friends"—not only illuminate how these relationships transpire at Prep; they reveal how other sites of learning might nurture similarly transformative relational norms to engender a culture of authentic and critical care (Antrop-Gonzalez & De Jesús, 2007; De Jesús, 2012; Valenzuela, 1999).

Prep is one of many NYC schools where transformed student–teacher relationships have led to more dignified and humane environments for youth. Many educational researchers have looked at programs and schools in New York City and the roles and importance of student–teacher relationships in transforming classroom and school culture, as well as student achievement. Among these are Winn's (2007) work on University Heights High School and the Power Writers, De Jesús's (2012) work on El Puente Academy for Peace and Justice, Bartlett and García's (2011) work on Gregorio Luperon High School, Tyner-Mullings' (2014) work on Central Park East Secondary School, as well as Shiller (2012) and Rivera-McCutchen's (2012) work on "City Prep" and "Bridges Institutes" (pseudonyms for two critical small schools in the Bronx).

Collectively, these examples reveal that public schools can be sites for transformative learning and successful educational attainment, particularly for youth who historically have been marginalized from schooling. This point is salient in a climate where educational policies are continually framed around notions of "accountability," despite research and data that repeatedly call these policies into question. The voices of former and current Prep students and examples of other urban schools finding success with similar models point to the reality that macro-educational policies cannot overlook the importance of establishing an authentic culture of relational care—one of several key features of HRE—in authentic school reform.

Nonetheless, it is also important to note that student–teacher relationships need to be maintained by boundaries, as the role of the teacher is ultimately to help the student achieve academic success. While Prep students often place familial and fraternal descriptors on their teachers, they also use a tone of respect when describing their teachers and repeatedly state that teachers held them to high standards, both academically and socially. These perspectives do not mean that teachers simply should befriend or strive to be recognized as equal to students. Rather, the thematic narrative of this chapter suggests that teachers need to apply the same standards of humanity to the young people they work with as to those in their own peer group. This behavior pattern is, ultimately, what students will value and it will help them succeed.

Leveraging off this chapter on relationship building, Chapter 5 will illustrate certain processes and mechanisms at Prep that specifically cultivate a culture of respect and acceptance for all. In particular, Chapter 5 examines how the school's Core Values frame students' intellectual and social interactions with peers and adults, and how explicit school expectations contribute to a sense of belonging, tolerance, community, recognition, and self-worth among the student body. Students suggest that this emphasis cultivates a safer environment where they learn to engage and confront issues among themselves rather than ignore issues and let them fester. In turn, students attribute to this culture of respect not only a positive school experience, but also a learning environment that engenders more academic engagement from them.

CHAPTER 5

The Components of Respect

Strategies to Build Tolerance, Empathy, and Community Across Generations

"How can you sum up your experiences at Prep?"
"I could be myself." —Ernie, Prep alumnus, age 21

When Shawn came in for an interview, he was as poised and confident as I remembered him as a student 5 years before. Shawn graduated from Prep in 2003 and during his 4 years at the school had regularly provoked, challenged, and tested limits with staff and students; it was not always an easy relationship. Yet, when he spoke in May 2007 at the Prep Ten Year Celebration, Shawn professed profound appreciation for the school—particularly for the level of tolerance and acceptance and for the ways others pushed him to be his best self. In retrospect, the only thing he would change, he said, was his own "attitude." Indeed, 12 separate alumni mentioned Shawn when they described Prep as a school that values tolerance, diversity, and acceptance, and as a "place to be yourself." In many ways, Shawn exemplified a typical student at Prep—he felt at home despite being an individual who challenged traditional norms. In Shawn's case, he opposed socially constructed gendered norms and boundaries at school, and while this may have challenged some students who were steeped in static gender roles and binaries, the school intentionally created an atmosphere where gender expression was valued and appreciated. While highlighting Shawn perhaps positions him as atypical, I believe Prep alumni had a different motive for referring to him. They wanted to describe a unique community of which they were a part for between 1 and 4 years, a community they described as more tolerant, accepting, and diverse than what they previously had experienced, and one that many alumni claim they have not found since. More important, they described Prep as a place where they could be themselves, and this, in turn, made school not simply tolerable, but desirable. These claims are important as students consider and imagine other ways of being, engaging, and living, in an otherwise racist, heteronormative, sexist, and transphobic world.

This chapter illustrates the importance of creating a culture of respect by centering human dignity in schools and provides suggestions regarding how to operationalize this aspect of HRE in school practice. While positive student–teacher relationships emerge even in hostile school climates, in this chapter I argue that explicit values-oriented frameworks and intentionality about school space can facilitate more humanizing and democratizing intellectual and social interactions among youth and adults. This approach, which manifests in the humanistic core of HRE, functions to proactively and distinctly counter the various ways a hidden curriculum, which tacitly maintains competitive and capitalist values, operates in schools (see Giroux & Penna, 1983; Greene, 1986).

To support my argument, I portray how students at Prep view the aspects of school culture that they describe as essential to their schooling experiences. These include a tolerant and accepting environment; a welcoming place; a heterogeneous, diverse, and intergenerational community; and a general tone of safety. Through interviews and rich descriptions of student engagement in school life, I show the ways that this type of respectful school culture permeates many quotidian interactions. I also present a few intentional school processes that infuse respect throughout the school, ultimately contributing to a sense of belonging, recognition, and self-worth among the student body. Because the school culture is grounded in structures and processes such as the Core Values framework and the Prep Central space, students learn to confront difference and issues among themselves (rather than let them escalate or ignore them and let them fester) in a safe and productive environment. I argue that by engendering an intentional heterogeneous, diverse, and intergenerational space in which all actors engage in humane, truthful, democratizing, respectful, and challenging discourse, students can participate more actively in academic and social aspects of school life. For these reasons, I contend that purposeful and unambiguous commitment to broader school culture and social ideals is a necessary, integral component of school reform. This prioritization is particularly important and salient in a time when school culture often is sidelined by narrow curricular and testing mandates, when zero-tolerance policies dominate school practices at large, and when school segregation remains incredibly high (Kucsera, 2014).

BUILDING ACCEPTANCE, EMPATHY, AND COMMUNITY: STUDENT PERSPECTIVES

Like most kids at most schools in New York City, young people at Prep come from a variety of backgrounds and have wide-ranging interests and passions. However, what came up repeatedly with current and former students was that there was no real dominant aesthetic or culture at Prep, and kids from seemingly different groups often intermingled and formed friendships freely. Epiphany, a 9th-grader, commented:

Prep is a place where you can be yourself. And that you don't have to worry about people talking bad about you, and saying, "Oh, do you see the way this person dressed?" You can dress how you want, and no one's gonna say nothing. They might say, "Oh, you're crazy for wearing that," but you can dress how you want, and no one can say anything. They can't say, "Oh, she dresses weird." It's not about style at Prep. It's not about the clothes you wear or the people you hang out with. It's your attitude. Like, if you had an [ugly] attitude, people are gonna think of you as someone not to talk to. But because Prep is so accepting and so inviting . . . you can actually have an attitude. (interview, March 2007)

As Epiphany noted, she did not feel as much pressure from her peers to dress or look a certain way because at Prep it was about "your attitude," the way one respected and treated other people. At the same time, she talked about feeling that she could be comfortable with herself even when she had an "attitude," because she was in an environment that was "inviting" and "accepting." She intimated that this was the ethos of the community.

Upon first glance, this may seem rather unremarkable. What does this have to do with school? Yet, students repeatedly mentioned how this aspect of school culture was fundamental to their experience (and success) at Prep. More important, this pattern is illustrative of an environment wherein each individual's humanity, worth, and role in the greater community are central priorities—and just as important as academic growth. Creating a welcoming, accepting, and community-oriented environment is not simply an additive measure to learning; these are fundamental aspects of school life that restore humanity (through valuing the multiplicities of identities of all students), build solidarity (empathy skills), and generate respect among students and faculty (for themselves and for one another).

An Accepting and Tolerant Environment

Like Epiphany and Shawn, Magdalena feels comfortable at Prep because she believes her ideas are respected and she can express them freely and safely. When talking about how Prep is different from her neighborhood and even her home, she states:

I feel like it's two different worlds, but I'm glad. You know, happy about that because when I'm at home, it feels that I'm trapped and I don't feel comfortable because, you know, people there tend to disagree from my views on issues. And when I'm in school it's like an escape from home, like, ahhhhhhhhhh, you know, it's like—I can, you know, be who I wanna be. (interview, March 2007)

Magdalena goes on to explain that she sometimes struggles at home and in her community because some folks are unwilling to accept her sexuality. She finds Prep to be a safe haven in terms of that aspect of her identity.

Sammy, an alumnus who had transferred to Prep after one semester at a prestigious public school, also spoke about being accepted and talked about how he could be himself because the school "tolerated him" (interview, April 2007). Specifically, Sammy mentioned that people often had mistaken his shyness for aloofness and arrogance, but at Prep he felt more understood. This is consistent with how Lisa, another alumna, describes being treated at her previous Catholic school and at Prep:

> It was just, like, you couldn't have your hair a certain way; you couldn't have so much jewelry or a certain kind of jewelry. And I felt that the school became focused on the kind of person you were and trying to control you . . . you couldn't go up these stairs, you couldn't do this. It was just ridiculous and I felt like they focused on it so much that they would actually punish you for it. They paid attention to stupid stuff like that. But I felt when I came here to Prep it was more of a liberal environment and, like, I felt that the school treats each one of the kids as an individual. And I think that's very important, especially when you're a teenager because you're getting . . . you know, there's so much going on during that time, and to constantly have people trying to tell you . . . to try to tell you, you know, be this way, be that way. You know, it's kind of stressful and kind of annoying. But at Prep I felt like . . . it felt like home and it was more just an egalitarian kind of setting. (interview, March 2007)

Lisa describes Prep as an "egalitarian" setting where "the school treats each one of the kids as an individual." In contrast, strict and punitive dress and behavioral codes in Catholic schools are mentioned as homogenizing practices; public schools often employ similar measures. For example, at the separate large high school—which at the time of the research occupied most of the space in the building where Prep is—students who wear hats or do-rags or bring any electronics are subject to detention or even suspension.

As Harry noted (explained in Chapter 3), one of the foundational reasons he started the school was that he and others felt restricted by and fundamentally against the rise of an excessively punitive culture that particularly targeted Black and Latino youth. As a result of the very different and more humanized approach at Prep, students describe feeling accepted as a member of the larger community. For most students and alumni, this feeling of being accepted also led them to accept others. Sammy suggests that interacting in a tolerant, respectful community that accepts the individual leads one to become more accepting of others:

I liked the people a lot. I liked the students and the teachers. Like, I don't know . . . I think the fact that the teachers didn't judge people because of stuff, like, trickled down to the students; so, the students were less judgmental of each other. And then people would accept . . . I don't know because it's hard to . . . there's a lot of people who are, like, have similar interests and can get along well. But they won't ever know it unless it's in the right circumstances, you know. And I think Prep is the right circumstances for a lot of people who wouldn't normally realize that they have stuff in common, to find out that they have things in common. It was very accepting and very, you know, like I said, nonjudgmental. Even stuff that was pretty out of the ordinary. Not that people wouldn't say anything about it . . . they would say something about it but they wouldn't give you a hard time about it. (interview, April 2007)

Reiterating the sense of acceptance that Epiphany described, Sammy further suggests that the teachers' general attitudes were infectious and students eventually picked up on the fact that inclusive acceptance of diversity was the norm. Sammy also sheds light on an interesting phenomenon: He describes a place where students were able to get to know one another and perhaps transcend differences they came to see as superficial.

Students and alumni often remarked about how racially integrated the school is, in contrast to their neighborhoods or previous schools, which were either strictly one ethnic or socioeconomic group or where groups often formed cliques bound by race. Monique, an alumna, notes and appreciates that Prep, beyond being diverse in its enrollment, was actually "really integrated." She says her small, elite, predominantly White and wealthy private liberal arts college in New England is not racially and socioeconomically integrated, despite its having a significant and increasing percentage of low-income students and students of color:

I feel like it's interesting how, although I talked a lot during my time at Prep, it kind of went under the radar when I came to [small, private New England liberal arts college]. I just didn't really talk as much in class. And I'm trying to do that, but I think it's . . . intimidation. . . . Although I'm in a different environment, which I thought wouldn't really affect me because I've been in a high school environment [Prep] . . . where there were White people. In high school there were, but I didn't mind that because it wasn't that big of a deal, but I guess to be removed away from the city environment, which I thought wouldn't affect me, has, because it's very, very different and it kind of makes me see how different New York City is from every other place and how people [attending the college] are different. (interview, March 2007)

Monique, who identifies as African American, is trying to work through the intimidation she feels about making herself heard in a schooling environment where she perceives non-White voices to be less valued and dismissed. She mentions feeling surprised that the change in setting has even affected her because at Prep she had been more or less comfortable engaging with White people, even if they disagreed.

Joshua, a 9th-grader, discusses how the community at Prep honors the individual without negating her or his group identities. He specifically couches this in terms of race:

> The students are interesting. Everybody has their own little personality: like, something is different about everybody. You'd be like, "Wow, like . . . he didn't do that! Like, okay." Like, everybody has something different about them so it's not all the same people. . . . But, I mean, we like and have respect for everybody. For different people . . . no matter what race. No matter anything. What color or nothing. (interview, March 2007)

It is important to note that when Joshua mentions, "no matter what race," he is not advocating a color-blind ideology, but rather a call to understand the intersectionality of students' identities, that there are multiple facets that define who they are. In fact, as will be discussed in later chapters, issues regarding race (and class, gender, etc.) in the school and beyond often were discussed, debated, and contested in many areas of school life. According to Fine, Weis, and Powell (1997), schools can—and should—create spaces that encourage intellectual and social engagements across racial and ethnic groups. Students suggest that this often happens openly and freely at Prep, where there are intentional spaces for intergenerational dialogue about issues of difference and identity.

A Welcoming, Safe Place

Given the denigrating experiences many students had in previous schools, Prep's welcoming community was fundamental to their students' overall (re) socialization and/or attraction to school. For instance, Paz, a senior, recalled:

> I think my most memorable time was probably the first day in the 9th grade, 'cause I was so nervous I didn't want my dad to leave me. I saw all these people here and I'm just sitting in Prep Central and then I got scared . . . but then . . . they [two older students] just started a conversation with me like, "Hi." . . . Yeah, everybody's just talking to me so I just felt instantly comfortable and I just felt good. 'Cause in my other school I was pretty shy and I saw a bunch of people, but I would never go up to anyone and be like, "Hi." Like, I would just sit there and wait for them to come talk to me. (interview, May 2007)

In this example, Paz specifically mentions how other, older students approached her and made her feel welcome at the school. According to many students, this hospitable environment made them feel happy and want to come to school, thus leading to increased academic engagement. Vivian, a senior, explained this in an interview as the most essential feature of schooling:

> To make them feel comfortable and make them feel like they're welcomed. I think that's the most important thing any school should do. And I think Prep does that very well. You know, make them feel like, "Hey it's okay to be in school." . . . It's not a place like where people are like, "I want to stay home every day." I think that's an important thing . . . they, like, say, "Hi. Welcome to school." I guess just talking to kids and letting them know, hey school can be fun. And I think that makes people feel welcomed. And they're not singling anyone out and, like, this is a bad person or anything. I also think the school has given me an environment that is easier for me to work in than in my old school. And, you know, they give me access to teachers if I need them, and supplies. And they just make things easier. And, you know, the school makes me feel safer and happier. (interview, May 2007)

There is so much to unpack in Vivian's statement. She describes the accessibility of the teachers at Prep, but she also associates feeling welcome with being happy and safe. Moreover, she makes specific reference to how she believes this is different from other schools. In fact, as Ray, a junior, explained in a focus group, "Kids are so happy to be here, they come!" (May 2007). Ray implies that students might not come to school when they feel alienated from the environment.

While this type of alienation from schooling is documented in a lot of literature about "dropouts," students who have not "dropped out" also are acutely aware of some of the processes that might push them out of schooling (see Eubanks, Parish, & Smith, 1997; Fine, 1991; Suh & Suh, 2007; Tuck, 2012). Prep was Chakasia's third high school; she said, "I feel more comfortable here, I wouldn't want to go to no other, 'cause I like it" (focus group, May 2007). Chakasia was on the verge of dropping out, but she came to Prep and found an atmosphere that made it easier for her to learn:

> I don't think Prep is really lacking anything. I think the way Prep is makes it easier for me to learn . . . you know how sometimes you gotta break things down the way you understand it, you know? That's what Prep does for me. I mean, I understood things in school, but it kind of made it easier for me. I enjoy school now, kind of, 'cause I probably wouldn't come. (focus group, May 2007)

When asked whether she enjoyed her previous school, Chakasia said:

> No, not at all. . . . It was more . . . too strict. Not too strict because
> you need structure, but it was just . . . lots of times it got on my nerves.
> Everything they did got on my nerves. I didn't like wearing a uniform; it
> was so easy to get strayed away from what you're in school for, pretty
> much. I don't think Humanities Prep is lacking anything; I like it. (focus
> group, May 2007)

Chakasia's statement echoes Lisa's memories about being disengaged when
she attended a Catholic school (see Chapter 3).

Even students who attended *only* Prep for high school recognized that
its unique and welcoming environment might keep students in school. For
example, Magdalena, a senior, explained that being at Prep greatly changed
her expectations of high school. In the following excerpt, she describes what
she imagined high school to be like while she was still in middle school,
based on what she saw happening among the youth around her:

> [I thought] that, you know, we just gonna . . . let it be, like, a hangout
> spot and like, you know, try to graduate and probably would drop out
> and do my GED or something. . . . I didn't expect to, like, find a . . . you
> know, somewhere I need to feel comfortable and where I can be myself
> and you know, actually, like, learn from here. Like, so . . . yeah, it's not
> what I expected. (interview, March 2007)

For Magdalena, being comfortable is essential to learning, and her comments point to the ways that a welcoming environment interrupts processes
that push kids out of school.

It is not surprising that an inviting environment that also emphasizes
tolerance and community is safer and less prone to violence. The school culture at Prep contributes to a sense of safety that helps define the interactions
of the community. For example, Luis, an alumnus, states:

> Oh, we got along. Everybody got along, I think. You know, there was,
> you know, I think one or two fights, but, you know, that . . . for me be-
> ing there 4 years, two fights is, you know, way under what I thought.
> You know, I hear kids [in other schools] that say they get into fights all
> the time, but, you know, since Prep is so small, you knew everybody's
> name, and you know . . . you had the Core Values, everybody, you
> know, ultimately got along with each other. (interview, March 2007)

Luis underscores the benefits of a small learning environment; however,
he also identifies the Core Values (described in a later section) that serve
as a benchmark by which the members of the school community negotiate

behaviors. Joshua, who attended a small middle school, echoes Luis's sentiment about the lack of fighting at Prep, but adds that issues tend to get resolved nonviolently:

> There are no problems right now. There are no fights. Like, if I went to my old school, there might not be fights inside but whenever you got outside somebody was talking about somebody that's gonna fight. Here, there are no fights. Everybody's cool if there is a problem. If there is a fight it's resolved in like 2 days. There are no problems. It's not, like, okay we have to go get guns and knives . . . none of that. (interview, March 2007)

Joshua suggests that the lack of physical violence at Prep is not merely a result of problems being sidelined for later, but indicative of a more healthy school culture in which issues are dealt with and confronted through communication. This observation mirrors Sammy's earlier comment that teachers' interactions with students trickled down to create an environment of tolerance and respect among students as well. Reneka affirms this:

> They [other schools] have a lot of fights. I think the only reason they have fights is because the teachers can't communicate with the students; it seems like the teachers are scared of the students. As long as they communicate like the teachers at Prep did, every high school in New York should be fine. But, they don't communicate, they treat the kids like just any other number and the kids feel that. That's why they take attitudes on the teachers, or they just want to fight all the time; they're aggressive. (interview, March 2007)

Although there were two fights during my year of fieldwork, most students still describe Prep as a school in which violence rarely occurred. Overall, students generally feel that the school is safe and congeniality is an expectation. Luis, who mentioned the lack of fighting, later commented:

> The atmosphere was, you know, sort of lighthearted. Like, you know, you knew that you had to go to class, but there was not . . . you know, sometimes you can feel a malicious vibe, you know, but that was never the case. Everybody, you know, I felt like the teachers even though they were having a bad day, you know, they would treat you, you know, fine. So it was pretty good. (interview, March 2007)

Since the teachers, even when trying to get students to class, respectfully engaged with them, it set the tone for mutual respect and what the Coalition of Essential Schools identifies as a common principle: "a tone of decency and trust" (see essentialschools.org/common-principles/). Indeed, students repeatedly describe a resounding culture of respect that goes beyond superficial niceties. Matthew, a graduating senior, suggests:

> I think that what I learned from this school is just about people in general and how people are with one another. Despite all of the problems that everyone has with one another in this school, you know how everybody talks about each other. But we're all stuck together though, no matter what happens, it's crazy . . . what somebody told you that that person said this about you . . . we always remain friends. That goes for everybody; we're stuck together. When it came down to it, we all have each other's back and I think that's a beautiful thing. We're all growing to be brothers and sisters in some kind of way; we're all close, it's crazy. . . . I'm gonna miss this school . . . I had a good experience in this school with people and friends and teachers and stuff like that. I don't think I will get this experience again towards people. (focus group, May 2007)

While Matthew invokes some of the familial themes treated earlier, he also describes remarkably how at Prep a general spirit of conviviality decreases any escalation of tensions when issues arise. Matthew does not deny that there are quibbles or gossip; yet he expresses how, at Prep, people transcend potential conflicts because they are part of a community that affirms the value of respect.

A Sense of Community

Prep's affable environment definitely increases the feeling of community and solidarity among students. Sebastien articulates how pervasive and systemic acceptance, hospitality, and warmth decrease feelings of alienation:

> I feel like if people come to this school they will actually feel a part of it, instead of just feel like they are entering a building for a few hours where they have no choice but to go and just leave afterwards. You know. 'Cause I know a lot of people who stay after school, including myself, just to be around and 'cause I enjoy being in this school so much. I think people will feel a part of something rather than just going to school, you know. It's a community and a school, that's what I think people would like most about it because the teachers are so inviting as people. And they are very welcoming. So, I really think that about the educational level too. Like, people . . . I feel, like, people will learn and being that the school is small, you know, like, teachers will keep up with people and they will know people on a deeper level. Instead of having thousands of students in one school, when you have a few hundred, I think that's actually better for students. (interview, May 2007)

While Sebastien explicitly connects "smallness" with being known on a deeper level, he also discusses being part of a community rather than just a school. Prep students are keenly conscious of the explicit social mission of the school, as well as the obvious academic aspects of the mission. In Sebastien's case, these two missions are inextricably linked, contributing to an expectation that in addition to "the educational level," school is also a site for democratic engagement and a culture infused with respect.

Similarly, Pedro's fondest memory crystallizes this community spirit and he articulates how Prep surpassed his previous expectations:

> The best experience I had, I guess it would have to be a cross between just, like, going to the ping pong club [an after-school activity] it seemed like every Friday. And also there was just one experience it is really, it is really odd. It is just, like, in 10th grade there was a huge blizzard and you just had, like, the whole school lined up on both sides of the street and just . . . you never see that with any other school. And that was something you never . . . that was something I'd never expected at school. . . . Yeah, just like a huge snowball fight, it is like the whole school and, like, just like, just regardless of, like, whatever feelings people had towards each other we were all, like, just, like, having fun that day. (interview, May 2007)

Pedro, who is an alumnus, does not suggest that everyone at Prep liked one another at all times; he acknowledges that there was sometimes friction. Yet, he also describes an environment in which people felt like part of a community, which he further describes as "something I'd never expected at school." Pedro speaks of a culture in which people respect one another and often even coexist happily together, regardless of "whatever feelings people had towards each other." He situates this as different from his previous experiences with schooling. As Magdalena noted, "Well, we all know each other and, like, you know, we all try to say hi to each other and you know, ask everyone how we doing and, I guess, we're . . . I don't know, like, really together, I guess. We all bond with each other or at least try to bond with each other (interview, March 2007). By acknowledging that tensions did arise among actors in the school and rapport was not always easy, Magdalena subtly acknowledges that the expectation of geniality tends to mitigate any escalation.

ENGENDERING A CULTURE OF RESPECT

The welcoming and tolerant atmosphere at Prep is not random, but thoughtfully integrated through many structures and processes that establish the school culture and ultimately support the academic aspects of the school. I will focus on two unique aspects of the school, the Core Values and Prep Central, which help solidify the respectful community that flourishes there.

Explicit Core Values

The Core Values at Prep serve as the moral fiber of the unique education the school intends to provide for its students. By framing the institution with these values, the school aspires for students to assimilate and exemplify them on campus and beyond. For instance, the following is an excerpt from the Student User's Guide, which couches the Core Values in the cultivation of community:

> What are Core Values? Prep is a community, not just a school. A community is a group of people who share common interests, concerns, and values. Being part of Prep is agreeing to share its Core Values: Respect for Humanity; Respect for Diversity; Respect for the Intellect; Respect for the Truth; Commitment to Peace; Commitment to Justice; Commitment to Democracy. Our rules and regulations are based on these Core Values. We want you to live up to them. You are encouraged to think about them as well. If in thinking about them, you believe a rule or regulation conflicts with our Core Values, you may through raising your issue at a Town Meeting or Advisory session—work to have them renegotiated.

While these values are normative, they are not necessarily teleological or static. In fact, they are framed as fluid in that students are expected to discuss, contest, and continually reflect upon them to understand their myriad meanings. In this sense, these values serve as a basis for a democratic institution that is evolving and changing, so that students can attach multiple and new meanings to the ideals that frame it. Moreover, as explicated in the Core Value Awards Guidelines, "We don't provide hard and fast definitions of the Core Values, since each of us lives them somewhat differently in our actions and our expectations of ourselves and others."

Prep uses many opportunities to integrate and discuss the Core Values in its comprehensive curriculum. As early as the first week of school, they are explained during orientation. Returning students are invited to share their perception of the school's Core Values with new students through skits, roundtables, and/or discussions. One year, I observed students "act out" the Core Values as silent statues for other students to guess (fieldnotes, September 2006). Often, classes are explicitly connected to a particular Core Value. For example, the course on Reconstruction was tied to the Core Values of Peace and Justice. Additionally, one year, a course called "Core Values in History" was taught at Prep. Course unit plans were aligned specifically to the Core Values (i.e., Commitment to Democracy looked critically at Imperial Athens by comparing it to U.S. Empire; Commitment to Justice compared restorative and retributive justice systems in the United States, in South Africa, and at Prep; and Respect for the Intellect was framed around the fact that the "Golden Age" in the Arab World influenced the European Enlightenment). Thus, the Core Values are not just written on paper, but also woven into various aspects of the curriculum. Students also discuss the Core Values in Advisory, the daily space for social and emotional well-being, and create schoolwide art projects based on them.

One of the most formal ways the Core Values are incorporated is through the End Term Ceremony. The End Term Ceremony, which happens twice a year at the end of each term, is a time for students and staff to stage performances, say goodbye, give speeches, and receive both academic awards and Core Value Awards. While the faculty ultimately decides by consensus which students receive the Core Value Awards, students in each advisory nominate two students for each Core Value in the categories of "Strong Commitment" and "Emerging Voice." During the process of student nominations, students are encouraged to think about and reflect upon the meaning of the Core Values. While other factors—including who has received awards and nominations in the past and who might receive an academic award—also are considered, faculty take student nominations very seriously.

Because there are numerous conscious efforts to infuse the Core Values of Prep into the school culture, students are familiar with them and talk about enacting them in informal ways. Related to the culture of care that manifests in and through various school relationships, many students articulate the importance of the Core Values in helping to create a culture that is fundamental to students' academic and social well-being at school. For instance, Sammy, an alumnus, explains that the Core Value of respect for the intellect contributes to students' sense of belonging in the school:

> Well, I mean, in terms of respect for the intellect, like, there's a lot of really intellectual stuff going on at Prep. Like, a lot of really good classes with things that might not be discussed in other classes in other schools. And respect to [sic] everybody's level of intellect, you know, just something . . . there's something for everybody to feel smart about. . . . I think the fact that the teachers didn't judge people because of stuff, like, trickled down to the students; so, the students were less judgmental of each other. And then people would accept [each other]. (interview, April 2007)

Linking the sentiments that classes at Prep are both inclusive and intellectual, Sammy suggests that this affects how students interact with one another. By being in a community that, as he describes it, accepts the individual (and her/his intellect and thoughts), Sammy posits that students feel less alienated and more connected to their peers and teachers than they previously could have imagined.

While most alumni could not remember all of them word for word, many suggested that the Core Values had some influence on their world-view. Students and alumni said that the Core Values provided a useful frame for interacting with others and that they had assimilated the Core Values in some way. For example, Vivian remarked:

> I think the Core Values are a good thing to have in a school because even though you might not see it . . . they're not just for school; they're for life. . . . Well, a lot of what I've learned here is just "be nicer and be more outspoken," and, you know, "don't be so shy," because I used to be a really shy person. I didn't talk to, like, anyone, and I guess that's helped me because I am a lot nicer to people. I do think twice before I wanna get mad at someone or I wanna, you know, use physical violence against them, and I guess that's a value that I've obtained while being at Prep. (interview, May 2007)

Here, Vivian described that the Prep Core Values are for life, suggesting that the explicit values-laden curriculum was just as important as the school's academic curriculum. In this sense, the school, by being forthright and clear about the values it wants students to assimilate, has made unambiguous what usually is considered a "hidden curriculum." Victor, a senior, stated:

> Like I said before, my thought process kinda changed [after coming to Prep] . . . now that I come here, I think about stuff more. Like I said, I look at all perspectives, and every which way. I guess I'm more, like, centered as a person . . . I guess I have peace with myself. I believe I have a meaning now, stuff like that. . . . I've always had an idea what I wanted to do with my life, but now, it's more clear-cut, and I know the type of environment I wanna be in and everything like that. . . . I think Prep is very welcoming. I don't think the school's for everybody. I mean, there are certain people that like the old-style school that you just learn something. Certain people learn that way. But I think that if you come to Prep, if you just basically . . . you don't even have to really follow the classes. If you basically follow the Core Values, then you will become a better person and learn more. (interview, May 2007)

Perhaps it would be a stretch to say that Victor feels more centered *because* of the Core Values; there are other factors that may have influenced him. Nonetheless, he does suggest that he knows he wants to be in an environment like Prep, framed by similar values. Internalization of the Core

Values may have inspired in him the hope that he can create or find this type of environment beyond the school.

Victor implies that he (and others) became a "better person" because he was challenged to "follow" the Core Values. Many students specifically acknowledged that Prep is unique because of its Core Values; as Victor stated, "All schools should have them!" (interview, May 2007). While some students did not mention Prep's Core Values explicitly, they invoked a similar discourse about how some features of "the school" made them "better people." The comments featured in Table 5.1, which came from interviews and focus groups, illustrate this point.

While ideals cannot *make* anyone better, Prep students and alumni consistently articulate another *purpose* of schooling beyond the academic. They all reference how the school pushed them to be their best selves. In Vaughn's case, he connects that to being valued, heard, recognized, and known. The aforementioned examples intimate that students consider the school's Core Values an essential part of their schooling.

In fact, in the following excerpt, Lisa made an explicit connection between the Core Values and everyday life:

> I think they [Core Values] are necessary because it's just a reminder that you as a . . . not just a student, but as an individual . . . that these are the things that you also take outside beyond school. And to have respect for . . . respect to diversity. I think these are the things that are just important, like, outside of school, as well. To start that in school, I don't know what I'm saying anymore . . . I guess to create that kind of foundation in school or in high school is important because then you take it with you for the rest of your life because high school is really important. I feel like it does have a big impact on what the person comes to be . . . sort of speak so as to have those Core Values. . . . I just feel they're important. It's, like, a reminder of what you need to do, what you should do. (interview, March 2007)

Whether perceived assimilation of these values has a transformative effect on students will be explored more deeply in Chapter 8, but respondents concur that everyone at Prep has to engage and make meaning of the school's Core Values—even if that means rejecting them.

Explicit Spaces for Humanizing Discourse: Prep Central and Intergenerational Exchange

While the Core Values frame the environment of the school, Prep Central is an intentional space that helps facilitate the humane and respectful tone of the school. Sitting in the largest room on the Prep side of the Bayard Rustin Complex, directly across from the school's main office, Prep Central is the

Table 5.1. Students Articulate How Prep's Core Values Were an Essential Part of Their Schooling

Name	Status	Quotation	Date
Reneka	Alumna	If I had gone to another school, I would have been in more trouble. Prep made me a better person by forcing me to understand more.	Interview, March 12, 2007
Vaughn	11th-grader	But I just think it's an effective school. It made me better and it made a lot of people better, I'm sure. I feel like a lot of people can learn here. It's not like a big school where, you know, your teachers don't really know your name. Or you don't know theirs. And it's just like, you come to school just to not get marked absent and you probably get marked absent because they probably don't see you. I just think everybody's heard. Everybody's seen. Everybody has an opinion and everybody listens. So I would recommend this school. Definitely.	Focus group, May 11, 2007
Magdalena	12th-grader	[about Core Values] It's really useful. I mean, it's something that we should use and, like, should practice it and it gets, like, something that would help us grow as students and also as people. And yeah, something that everyone should practice, I think.	Interview, March 21, 2007

first room that visitors usually see. While layout does not allow this room to be located in the actual center of the school, Prep Central is central enough to be "where just, like, the whole school really came together at times," according to Pedro, an alumnus (interview, May 2007).

In Prep Central, teachers share their workspace with students. This set-up for their desks, according to many teachers, aligns the space with Prep's mission to create "an atmosphere of informal intellectual discourse among students and faculty" (see Appendix B). Clarissa, a music teacher, explains the relationship between this space and the mission of the school:

Prep Central was the first place that I saw when I came to the school and I was struck by the level of intimacy between the students and teachers in the space. I feel that having a space dedicated to that type of interaction is in line with the mission, particularly [students] having good connections with adults. (interview, April 2006)

Andrea, a math teacher, echoes that sentiment by explaining, "The sense of community that kids still feel, you know, when they go in Prep Central or in the school, feels OK, feels fine" (interview, March 2007).

Students offered similar descriptions about their experiences in Prep Central and described it as an essential feature that made the school unique. For instance, at Alumni Days[1] in both 2006 and 2007, several students, when invited to give feedback at the staff meeting, said that Prep Central was one space that must be preserved. Each time they came back to visit the school, they were concerned that Prep Central had been moved, sometimes into smaller rooms. Alumni did not realize that this was because the school continually was forced to move into other locations and many decisionmakers who were outside of Prep felt that Prep Central was an extraneous space. Alumni concerns about maintaining the space are a clear indication that Prep Central was fundamental to their experience in the school.

For most students, Prep Central was the place in the school where they could relax and be with their friends. Marianna, an alumna, remembered it as a place to "take naps on the couches" (interview, 2007). As a student who was in and out of group homes during her time at Prep, she described the place as a refuge, as well as a place where she could converse and hang out with friends. When Shawn, another alumnus, was asked what he liked best about the school, he shared, "You know, the best conversations ever, the best. I miss Prep Central" (interview, May 2007). Clearly, for Shawn, Prep Central represented more than a room; it was a place to build upon relationships and interactions with friends.

For others, forming friendships was important, but Prep Central also allowed them to experience (and to imagine) something they might not have experienced elsewhere. According to Jenkins, a recent alumnus:

Yeah, I believe every school is the same in that you go to your class and do your work. But every school has a different approach to that environment, and I would say that this school has a really unique approach. I always used to tell my mom that I always used to think of this school as, like, the school for the coolest hippies in the world. Like Woodstock, you know, making music and doing what you gotta do. I used to tell my mom about, uh, Prep Central; you can sit on a sofa. That right there, that's the image of college that I saw, you come out of your class, you go sit on the couch, drink a coffee or something, talk with friends, play chess, we did that here too, read a newspaper, study, go to computers, you know. Those images, yeah, yeah. (interview, March 2007)

In his description, Jenkins not only talks about the many ways Prep Central was used, but he ascribed a "college-like" quality to it, suggesting the space inspires hope and possibility about the future through what is happening in the present. Moreover, he reaffirms how relationships in all forms (academic, social, even musical) were cultivated and experienced in this space, and that students were treated as intellectuals and artists. This echoes what Dalia, another alumna, said when she remembered that she learned to play guitar from her peers in the space. Because it is designed as a shared workroom, Prep Central formalizes the transformative relationships and culture of respect between and among students (discussed in Chapter 4 and in this chapter). For example, Alejo, another alumnus, shared how this crystallized the commitment to equalizing and democratizing relationships between and among students and teachers, and how this was different from his previous school:

> Well, for one . . . the lounge. There is no other high school in the city that has that [students and teachers combined] . . . as long as the students can go in. 'Cause normally what it is, is you're either in class or you're eating lunch, or you're in class, or you're home, or outside of the school with peers; but there's no real interaction between students and teachers. (interview, April 2007)

In this discussion, Alejo described how school design generally alienates students from teachers, whereas at Prep, through the advent of Prep Central, relationships, discussions, and community were embraced and facilitated. In this sense, even if a teacher did not have lunch with students, talk to students informally in the hallways, or try to form personal connections with students, she/he was still forced to reconsider traditional student–teacher interactions because her/his workspace was intentionally shared with students.

Other students pointed to how this official space contributed to transforming relationships among students. For instance, Erin, an alumna, stated:

> Yeah, I think it was great that it was a smaller school because in another place, I would never see the punk rock kids hang out with the kids who are more like a hip-hop, rap group. You know, those with the baggy pants with the Goths, but in Prep, you sit down in . . . the lounge area. You have all various groups just sitting down there talking to each other. You have just some people playing chess with each other. I kind of miss that. (interview, May 2007)

Many students appreciated the diversity and friendships that happened at the school across various racial and socioeconomic lines. Even if a school is small, if there are not communal spaces beyond the classroom for students to get to know one another, students may remain segregated based on characteristics such as clothing style, country of origin, or race. Moreover, Erin explained that she has not encountered the same level of tolerance and cohesion in her college:

> I think that sometimes I tend to wish things were like Prep . . . I liked the fact that we talked about certain topics. The people that I was hanging out at SUNY with really didn't care for those types of things. I really wanted to share my opinion with people who did care. . . . And then, it's not all Black people [at SUNY]. There's a lot of White people. . . . The thing is that when I was there at SUNY, a lot of people are like, "Well, just hang out with the Black kids; don't hang out with the White kids." But I felt like I had gotten more experience . . . [from Prep] interacting with people outside of my normal people that I would usually hang out with. I felt like I learned more and I think they learned a lot from me, too. (interview, May 2007)

Erin describes the difficulty of creating a diverse community of friends at her college in upstate New York, a theme I will expand upon later. Nonetheless, because of her positive experience at Prep, where she learned firsthand that interacting with peers of different races is possible and desirable, Erin aimed to make this happen, despite finding herself in a much more segregated environment. As Rodriguez and Conchas (2008) point out in their study on small schools, strong social relationships form among students from different backgrounds when they are supported and encouraged to work together by the school staff. However, this cannot be assumed to happen automatically at a small school, especially given the social contexts of racism, hetero-patriarchy, and white supremacy that exist alongside schooling. The examples from students and teachers at Prep show that integrated spaces for informal discourse among all students and staff foster a heterogeneous and intergenerational community—and such spaces are critically important, particularly as New York State is criticized for having the most segregated schools in the country (Kucsera, 2014).

In addition to operating as a setting for intergenerational dialogue across difference, Prep Central serves as a safe locale for meaningful, spontaneous conversations between students only. For instance, one afternoon, after school hours, I encountered 10 students on the couches in Prep Central having an animated conversation about the meaning of grades and a "good" education:

> They were having what seemed to be an animated discussion about the school, and what made it a "good school" or not. There was much banter about doing "seat time" and "actually learning" and indulging in one's education. The discussion seemed to get deeper when one of the

students asked, "Should you get a good grade if you are not pushing yourself to grow?" (fieldnotes, December 2006)

I had come in to get some papers and was not "formally observing," but I was pulled in by what the students were saying. Normally, because of the culture of the school, I might have jumped right in and offered my thoughts, but I decided to see where they would go with it themselves. Similarly, another day I walked into a conversation unfolding in Prep Central about "philanthropy." The following excerpt is from my fieldnotes:

> In Prep Central, some students were having a very lively and vociferous conversation about philanthropy . . . whether or not money should be donated or whether students should fundraise. Apparently, they were brainstorming on how to get their trip to New Orleans subsidized. Some of the students in this group were going down for spring break to help build houses with teachers. I could not stay long to hear it all, but the conversation grew increasingly more intense; it shifted from one about fundraising for the trip to something about "activism versus philanthropy." Victor was defending corporate philanthropy, arguing that "we live in a capitalist society and we might as well make the best of it." Sebastien, however, was saying that ultimately corporate philanthropy would not change the situation for people of color or folks that were poor. He said that "doing something" to change the structure would. In many ways, this reminded me of the types of discussions that transpired in my graduate education and development classes. (January 2007)

As a formal place to hold informal conversations, Prep Central serves in many ways as a vehicle for students to feel comfortable around one another and as a way "to find their voice and to speak knowledgeably and thoughtfully on issues that concern their school, their world" (see Appendix B). While there was no fixed "outcome" to either of these discussions, students were engaging in critical dialogue without the "help" of any particular teacher. These conversations demonstrate that students not only had a place to go after school, but also had a place to engage in critical dialogue with other students. Because Prep honors this space as one "for informal intellectual discourse among students and staff," it becomes a place for collective dialogue and relationship building among all members of the community, whether students or teachers. As discussed in Chapter 4, students and alumni valued the types of interactions they had with their teachers and also appreciated having regular opportunities to dialogue and get to know other students, particularly students they might have had a hard time getting to know in another schooling environment.

Interestingly, some alumni described their conversations and experiences in Prep Central as an extracurricular activity. For example, when asked about what students participated in "after school," both Kevin and Deena noted that they went to Prep Central. Kevin noted that Prep did not have many structured extracurricular activities, but he said that "Prep Central and the after-hours culture there made up for it." He felt that "there were a lot of definite social outlets and quite frankly, I did not even want to go home" (interview, December 2007). In some ways, this points to how the school has integrated formal structures that may have removed the need for formalized extracurricular activities often deemed necessary in traditional schools. While there were definitely some after-school activities at Prep, students stayed in Prep Central beyond school hours to talk, play chess, receive tutoring, or play music. While traditional notions of civic education posit that an increased extracurricular program leads to democratic engagement (Hart, Donnelly, Youniss, & Atkins, 2007), Prep integrates elements of democratic education into the day-to-day school culture and curriculum so that supplemental structured after-school activities are less necessary. This is particularly important because, in reality, some Prep students might not have been able to take advantage of such activities and experiences if they were available only in the context of formal after-school programs.

CONCLUSION: THE CASE FOR FINDING PLACE AND CREATING SPACE

These rich student testimonies show how the respectful school culture at Prep permeates many of the students' interactions in the school. The explicit values framework helps infuse respect throughout the school, ultimately contributing to a sense of belonging, tolerance, community, recognition, and self-worth among the student body. In the context of a school culture grounded in humanizing core values, students learn to confront and work through differences and issues among themselves as they struggle to understand and enact the meaning of the Core Values, even in a world that does not often embrace them. Further, Prep Central—an intentional heterogeneous and intergenerational space—gives all members of the school community opportunities to spontaneously engage in humane, truthful, democratizing, respectful, and challenging discourse. The Core Values and Prep Central are undeniably pivotal to students' experiences at the school and not simply add-ons to the school's academic and democratic curriculum.

James Baldwin and Harvest Collegiate high schools also ground their school cultures in core values. El Puente Academy for Peace and Justice uses the Sankofa Curriculum, which is ultimately a values framework, to guide how students engage with one another in the schooling environment. Although many schools do not have the space or resources to create a room like Prep Central, a few other schools demonstrate exemplary ways that physical space can be configured to facilitate a positive school culture.

Urban Academy, for instance, has an entryway framed with student art-work and photography, warmly inviting visitors, students, and families into the school. Upon climbing the staircase, one enters a large lobby where one might find students and teachers talking on one of the many sofas strewn throughout the room. Adjacent is a shared teacher and student workspace that is buzzing with conversation and activity. At Harvest, the large entry room on the first floor houses a piano. It is not uncommon to hear music filling the halls between classes, or clusters of students engaged in meaning-ful conversations about schools, relationships, or the world. The vastness of the entry room space contributes to enabling these types of exchanges at Harvest.

In subsequent chapters, I discuss in more detail how the academic cur-riculum and participatory democratic spaces at Prep (e.g., Town Meetings, Fairness Committee, etc.) are thoughtfully woven throughout multiple areas of school life to solidify the transmission of the school's values-based culture and enable the meaningful student–teacher relationships and culture of care and mutual respect outlined in this chapter and Chapter 4. These approach-es are integrated and they all contribute to establishing the school culture. In fact, these approaches are essential in laying the groundwork for students to participate more actively in academic and social aspects of school life, which is why they must be integral to school reform efforts.

CHAPTER 6

The Components of Critical Questioning

Building a Culture of Curiosity, Intellectualism, and Activism

One of the more popular electives at Prep, "Parenting," can be taken for either health or English credit. The essential question for the course is simply, "What makes a good parent?" In order to help students answer this question throughout the semester, the teacher integrates materials and theories from a variety of disciplines and perspectives, including literature, psychology, and health. Below is an excerpt from my fieldnotes describing one of the Parenting classes:

> The students enter the classroom at a leisurely pace as Tania, the teacher, is writing on the board. She is over-viewing the assignment that was due: Memoir, Themes, and Life Theme. She then passes out work to the students who are still coming in. As kids still settle in, she says things like, "Come in, my brother in-law," which reflects a friendly, welcoming atmosphere. She then gives them 2 minutes to get notebooks out and to get organized and then says, "You will then have 5 minutes to write about your dreams."
>
> It still takes students time to settle down, as they are still wound up from lunch. Tania goes around to each one, to help them settle and get on task. They are either doing a timeline of childhood, writing about three memories, or working on one memory. She reminds them that the next assignment will be on pleasure and pain. Overall, it is a very inclusive environment, both with curricular content and the pedagogical methods. Both are personalized. Students are still coming in later, but as most of the class is working, they immediately settle in. Tania continues to go around and offers encouraging comments to students individually. I overhear her say to Gio, "This is brilliant and totally insightful," while pointing to three specific examples in the free-write. She also connects with him personally by saying that her partner does something similar in his approach to writing.

Most students are writing diligently, and a few of them begin to share their memories among themselves. Many of them want to tell the teacher their memories, which prompts her to say, "You guys are bursting at the seams—you are almost ready to share." The class is then talking to each other informally, mostly sharing memories. There is a very informal aspect to the class, but students are continually working. She finally lets them know that they should end their free-writes. She instructs the students to do a whip around, and to say two words about how they are feeling. Student responses run the gamut: nostalgic, depressed, hyper, rejected, good.

At this point, Tania begins to ask the volunteers to share their stories. Vaughn volunteers first. He tells a story that takes place in 7th and 8th grade, when he wore his hair in "a long, big Afro." He told the class that he was really proud of his hair and felt like a lion. The girl behind him in class took her chewed gum one day and put it in his hair. He was so enraged that he slapped her. When he got home, his mom slapped him for slapping the girl, but then realized what had happened to his hair and tried to fix it. He then had a funny Afro, so he went to the barber. The barber shaved his head, so his hair was short. While he was sad to lose his hair, he said that he left feeling like a new person.

At this point, the teacher asks the students what they think the theme of this memory is. There is a lot of cross-talk, and many chime in on the theme, specifically wanting to know if he sought revenge. Then someone jumps in and says, "It seems you were king and then you were dethroned." Vaughn seems to appreciate this analysis.

Many stories ensue and students share. Randa tells the last story of when she was in 9th grade and she decided to wear her dad's clothes to school—his football jersey and baggy jeans. She wanted to see how it felt. She remarked that one Prep student thought she was a new student. Keenya then exclaims: "You were a dude for a day?" Randa: "Basically!" Magdalena: "The theme is gender bending and exploration!" Randa: "It felt good to wear his clothes." Vaughn: "I feel like you were exploring yourself but actually trying to say that you are Randa regardless." Susie: "Maybe you wanted to get noticed because you are a freshman." Bobby: "Maybe you were trying to feel like what it was to be your parent." At this point Randa says to Bobby, "Exactly!" and then the class is over. Tania reminds them that the following day, they will look at theory. As she is leaving, Keenya exclaims, "I enjoyed this class *very* much." (February 2007)

This snapshot captures the essence of Prep classes and, in many ways, the spirit of Prep itself—a warm, inviting, democratic, and vibrant environment in which student ideas are valorized, shared, and challenged. I share this particular excerpt because it illustrates several of the elements that students described as essential to their academic engagement at Prep: the in-depth and thematic nature of classes, the discussion-based environment, and strong emphasis on students' experiences and real-world application. Furthermore, the Parenting class is designed to be interdisciplinary, students' ages and abilities are intentionally heterogeneous, and primacy is given to project-based assessment and the use of sources over textbooks. The goal of the course, according to Tania, is "to provide students with a possible lens to think about the world" (interview, June 2007). Throughout my observations, I found that the Parenting class engaged students on deeply personal levels while also engaging them with social theory. My fieldnotes show that the students exhibited a level of comfort and safety in sharing very personal things about themselves, which not only built community in the classroom, but also did push them to think about their place in the world.

For instance, Victor talked about how the Parenting class, in particular, challenges him to think differently about himself:

> The classes at Prep are very, very different. I have a health class right now that's about parenting. You'd think it sounds like the classic high school Parenting class, like I have to hold a plastic baby in my hand, or something like that, and take it home so it doesn't get messed up, but it has nothing to do with that . . . you don't only learn, like, how you should raise somebody, because you learn more about yourself, I think, in that class, too . . . and about why you possibly are the way you are, like how your childhood affects you as an adult, or as a human being in general. You learn about how everything affects you. (interview, May 2007)

Similarly, Queenia, who took the class several years before, credits this class with making her more aware of herself and her decisions and outlook as a parent:

> I credit Prep with being the reason why I think I'm a good mother. . . . I took Parenting and it was not at all what I expected, Parenting. Like, I thought it was, like, the fake babies and the eggs but it was . . . right—it was more like the psychology of being a parent. I feel like I'm so much more aware of . . . kind of what I say affects my daughter and what she has . . . and how the tiniest little things that you don't think matter, shape their whole personality. Like, I'm so aware of that now and I'm so glad that I am because I see the way that other parents go through kids or the way that other people behave and I see it as a direct result of what they learned at home. I'm so glad . . . she's not going to be perfect, but I'm going to mess up and I'm going to make my mistakes, but I feel

like I'm not going to make the same mistakes I would if I didn't have that information. (interview, May 2007)

In both passages, the students distinguish this class from parenting classes in other schools where students are forced to participate in rituals such as carrying a baby doll or an egg—rituals they suggest lack meaning. These students' positive reaction to their Parenting class at Prep provides a snapshot of why students tend to feel comfortable, curious, and engaged in their classes at the school.

While the earlier chapters of the book lay the foundational elements of creating a school culture embedded in human dignity, I explore in this chapter how the academic curriculum at Prep also mirrored and furthered this process. Strong student–teacher relationships and a culture of respect clearly permeate the school, ultimately increasing students' academic engagement and helping define classroom practices. As Jenkins, an alumnus, noted, there is a connection between feeling comfortable at school and an increasing desire to perform academically: "Okay, the overall atmosphere was chilled. But chilled enough to make you want to do work. Kind of balances itself out" (interview, March 2007). Indeed, the pattern that emerged from my data is that the current and former students and the teachers who participated in this study consistently mentioned feeling academically engaged by the approach to critical questioning that undergirded the academic curriculum. Thus, in this chapter, I lay out the intentional classroom practices and curriculum approaches that define most classes at Prep—inclusive conversation, inquiry-based design, culturally and socially relevant content, heterogeneous groupings, and project-based work. Collectively, these reflect and help advance the principles and goals of HRE in terms of pedagogy and content, and normalize curiosity, intellectualism, and activism in the academic space.

HRE is a framework that intellectually invigorates and challenges students through engagement, and most alumni from schools that enact HRE feel extremely confident about actively engaging in their discussion-based social science and humanities classes in college. On the flip side, I highlight some challenges regarding Prep's constructivist, student-centered math programs, as some alumni questioned whether the program was sufficiently rigorous for college preparation. Because this tension may surface deeper questions about the "academic costs" of HRE, I share a few concrete ways to bridge HRE and math education to engender students' postsecondary success without sacrificing integral participatory processes. I offer suggestions and strategies for schools and teachers to address this issue and tension more deeply, so they do not lose the constructivist nature of their program as they consider ways to prepare students for all facets of postsecondary work and schooling.

STUDENT-TEACHER RELATIONSHIPS THAT PROMOTE
DEEPER ENGAGEMENT IN THE CLASSROOM

The caring and equalizing relationships between students and teachers at Prep described in Chapter 4 translate into deep and consistent engagement in the classroom. Most students described their teachers communicating in ways that made learning more accessible. According to Deena, an alumna who was attending a small liberal arts college in upstate New York:

> The teachers at Prep were awesome. I wish that there were more Prep teachers at my school [college] . . . What I like most about the teachers is that they are all really fun . . . speak to students really well . . . and it is hard to be a teacher and it is hard to be a teacher that makes the classroom fun, and I feel that from my experience at Humanities Prep, the classroom was fun! (interview, December 2006)

Others, like Alejo, an alumnus, commented on how teachers were incredibly knowledgeable in their areas of expertise as well as in other areas. According to Isaiah, a recent alumnus, this level of passion makes classes interesting because the teachers are committed to their disciplines. For instance, he stated:

> I'd say the teachers are very motivated and also very serious about what they're teaching. I think that if I can assume something about the hiring process and interviewing process, it's very . . . very selective. You seem to not have a lot of . . . not have a lot of inexperienced, you know, unmotivated teachers. Actually, you wouldn't have . . . I'd say you have none. I haven't . . . I haven't been here for a year, but I . . . I'd say it's probably still the case. (interview, March 2007)

Isaiah pointed out that in his old school, "teachers, even if they wanted to, were not allowed to teach . . . what they really felt passionate about" (interview, March 2007). According to students, the level of passion that some teachers at Prep exhibit about their subjects has a positive effect on student learning.

As described in Chapter 4, current and former students mentioned Prep teachers' care for students' academic well-being as something that increased their academic engagement. Reneka, an alumna, described the classes as "fun, always small; you got the help you needed, and if you didn't there was always the after-school programs. The classes were perfect" (interview, March 2007). She links her academic engagement with fun and the support she received. Academic support manifests, according to students, in teachers' willingness to give extra academic assistance, both during and beyond class time. For instance, Richie, a current senior, described his most memorable learning experience:

> I feel my most memorable learning experience was as a freshman: I had Mark at that time and he had given us a book . . . and he told the class to read the first 15 pages of the book, so I did that, and after reading the first 15 pages I completely got nothing. I really didn't get nowhere with it. So . . . and I probably figured there will be a couple people in the class who will get something out of it, so I was just looking for other people's feedback and surprisingly nobody really got anything out of it. So it was kind of a challenge for everybody. I just kind of figured I was a freshman so . . . but it was a very hard book. Also, Mark went through the book with us, but you know I took the extra time to go after school to Mark and we kind of read the book together. And we kind of made sense of the book together, you know. But at that time, it would really take like 2 hours of his time, really, on me, after school, so I kind of felt appreciated in a way and I never felt that . . . I didn't know a school would be like that. But it helped me understand the book a lot more than I did originally reading it, so . . . that was my most memorable. (focus group, May 2007)

In this passage, Richie describes how he counted on both his fellow students and teachers to help him comprehend the material, especially when he was struggling with it. He also explains how the extra time put in after school to make "sense of the book together" made him feel validated and appreciated, and ultimately helped him understand the material.

Several students noted that some teachers were amenable to student input in creating or changing the direction of classes. In many ways, this spoke to how students often feel validated at Prep, or at least taken into consideration by some of their teachers, mirroring the general culture of trust that transpired between students and teachers (described in Chapter 4). For example, Sandra, a senior, described how she confronted her math teacher about what she felt was wrong with the class:

> In my junior year I took math with Andrea, elective math. And I went up to Andrea while she was playing the guitar and I was like, "Excuse me I want to say something to you. Can you stop for a second?" and she started to laugh. And I was like, "I don't like your class." She was like, "What's wrong with it?" And I was like, "Everything you give me, I get it done within like seconds or minutes." And she was like, "Right." So I was like, "So why don't you teach us something like trigonometry or something? Do something like that?" And she did end up changing some things. (focus group, May 2007)

While Sandra did not explicitly state that she felt heard, she definitely described how the teacher listened to her suggestions and seemed to take them into account. Vivian, a senior, described a similar process when asked what she liked best about Prep:

> I love how the classes are designed. And I love how you can put your input, you know, in classes. And, you know, like . . . how teachers actually do like you. "Hey what do you like about that class? What do you not like? What do you think should be changed?" Like, when I was in a class with Mark, I was in his Dystopia class. And no one really liked *1984* or, like, part of the class didn't like it. So, we told him that and then next year he actually explained that, you know, the class didn't really like reading one book all together. So, you know, after that he gave us choices of books and that showed me that he was really listening. (focus group, May 2007)

In this case, Vivian described that she felt that her teacher, Mark, was "really listening." Later, when she described what she tells others about Prep, she explained how this level of input leads her to feel "happy":

> I tell them that the classes . . . although they are designed by the teacher, you know, we get some input too sometimes and that, you know, I'm more happy. I tell them, "Oh, I'm actually happy to get up and go to school in the morning." (focus group, May 2007)

Vivian depicted how her contributions to her own learning made her feel better about school, which ultimately brought her to a higher level of engagement. Isaiah, an alumnus, couched this in discourse about community, reinforcing how the culture of respect among teachers and students translates into the classroom and manifests in teachers sometimes letting students pursue individual interests within the class:

> Okay. I think what I like most about . . . I won't decide what I like most. What I like about Prep is . . . is . . . is the sense of community that's actually between teachers and students, the freedom that a student can get. Example: I was in a history class Tania was teaching. And I wanted to . . . I wanted to study the Irish civil rights movement in Northern Ireland while in class, the suggested topics were, like, the civil rights movement in the United States, the women's rights movement, or the anti-Apartheid in South Africa. Well, I was allowed to write about another topic, which was this one. (interview, March 2007)

While Isaiah frames his freedom to choose his own topic in "the sense of community," even though it is about individual pursuits, students also describe how they are encouraged to build off one another's work in the classroom, even as they work on their own. For example, Sammy, an alumnus, remembers:

> And I really like Javier's art class because he would play music and you could just . . . he might give you a little subject or theme for the day but then you could just pretty much do your own thing. Then everybody would get up and look at everybody else's stuff. That's what I'm saying. You're free to move around and there's a lot of collaboration, which is good. (interview, April 2007)

Sammy's description is suggestive of how the sense of community and allowing for individual pursuits are often in balance.

Pedro, an alumnus who attends a 4-year CUNY school, describes how the sense of community and the ways teachers deal with students at Prep reminds him of college:

> They [the classes] were very similar to college, like what you experience in college . . . and they were very inclusive. The faculty didn't act like they were above the students or knew better than the students. They really accepted their opinions from all points. (interview, May 2007)

Pedro's description resonates with earlier depictions of how student–teacher relationships at Prep are perceived to be symmetrical and help create classroom environments where student knowledge is valued and validated. Pedro describes this in a positive light, suggesting that the ways students and teachers interacted in the classroom normalized practices of academic engagement.

It is important to point out that students did not feel that every teacher at Prep used this approach. Throughout my interviews with current students, there were repeated complaints that two teachers in particular were not "Prep-like." When we discussed why, students explained that these two teachers were not particularly strict or demanding, but they taught in a traditional manner that was less inclusive and less applicable to students, and students did not feel as intellectually valued or engaged in classes with these teachers. These exceptions thus show the standard in terms of what "constitutes" a Prep teacher; as far as students are concerned, how teachers relate to students in the classroom clearly influences students' level of academic engagement.

CURRICULUM DESIGN: PEDAGOGIES, CONTENT, AND EXPERIENCES
THAT PREPARE STUDENTS FOR LIFE AFTER HIGH SCHOOL

Students were extremely specific about ways in which pedagogy and content reinforce and augment student engagement at Prep. The curriculum and pedagogies they described—hands-on, applicable, in-depth, thematic classes that could be tailored to be culturally relevant—reflect the type of humanizing classrooms that are central to HRE. In addition, heterogeneous groupings and opportunities to learn outside Prep are strategies that better prepare students for success in postsecondary schooling and work environments.

Relevant, In-Depth, Thematic Classes

Students and alumni repeatedly described their classes as being hands-on and applicable beyond the classroom. For example, Sammy spoke about how his Spanish class was practical, useful, and applicable:

> I liked . . . Spanish class. That was good. I liked that one a lot. I mean, I still remember some of the stuff we actually did and some of the activities we did in that class. And when we went to the coffee shop, La Taza de Oro, to order everything in Spanish. That sticks out in my head. I remember more from that Spanish class than my college one, where we didn't do anything like that. (interview, April 2007)

Sammy describes how these practical experiences engaged him in learning and helped him retain knowledge. His description shows how classes at Prep depart from standards-based curricula that emphasize rote memorization of content over practical applied skills. In fact, Sammy specifies that he retained more from practically applying his knowledge than from a more standard, content-oriented class.

Some students compared this approach with their old schools. Dalia, who briefly attended a large mainstream public high school, said:

> I was at [large public high school] my freshman year, and I just didn't feel . . . the education level was actually not so bad, it was the environment that I found kind of stifling. Even though I separated myself from the rest of my environment there, I just didn't feel that it was stimulating or even the people around me were stimulating enough. But, I guess it comes down to me . . . you know, it's just day in and day out, you study your subject and then you're out, but there was no depth to it and that's what I was looking for. (interview, February 2007)

At first glance, Dalia seems to blame those around her for not being stimulating and almost adopts a more meritocratic lens to school achievement ("it comes down to me"). However, she goes on to describe something more structural about school design and educational policy that led to an alienating and unstimulating environment. Isaiah, an alumnus, noted that, at his old school, the emphasis on breadth over depth led to disengagement:

> Coming from [large public high school], I was very unsatisfied with having, like, an overstuffed class of about 30 or more. I also felt that— that administrators at this school were not treating us with the same— with, like, inadequate amount of seriousness. One thing that I noticed is that—at a lot of the other schools I've been to—is that each class . . . you might get a few more details, but it's not a lot learned. . . . Here [at Prep] we explore topics and themes in far more depth. (interview, March 2007)

Isaiah was looking for a more critical education. Although he was actually quite successful at his previous high school, he did not appreciate the academic school culture or the atmosphere. He went on to say that "the classes tend to be more . . . thematic subjects than, like, General History class. You know, [a class called] War and Peace instead of 1500 A.D. to Today. And in one English class I had we just looked specifically at *Don Quixote*" (interview, March 2007).

Numerous students mentioned that the in-depth, thematic nature of classes at Prep allow students to engage more deeply with the material and with one another. For example, Shawn, an alumnus now at SUNY Albany, states:

> The Into Africa class . . . and the religion [Paganism and Monotheism] class . . . I think those were . . . my best classes that I remember because we went in-depth on specific subjects. I think we would choose a topic and then really look and focus on the topic. And everybody was involved and everybody had something to say and it didn't matter whether your answer was right or wrong, it was still part of the cumulative value of why we're looking at that topic. (interview, May 2007)

Shawn describes why he feels that depth allowed for more inclusion. Moreover, he echoes earlier sentiments of how student opinions were validated, even if a student was "wrong," because that answer became part of the "cumulative value of why we're looking at that topic." Bartlett, in her 2005 study of an adult literacy program in Brazil, notes that egregious abdication of the power to interrupt grave misconceptions is problematic and can be the downside of Freirean-type pedagogy. She illustrates how teachers frequently sought to validate students' knowledge—highlighting how teachers sometimes knew a student's comment was inaccurate but refrained from contradicting students. Shawn, however, seems to be describing something different. He illustrates how students engage with teachers and with one another to gain deeper, more personal understanding of an issue. He alludes to the spirit of debate and questioning, with students exchanging ideas and opinions on an issue, regardless of whether it gets resolved. The teacher or other students could disagree and even contradict; however, students felt their opinions were valued and encouraged. Thus, Shawn describes a relationship in the classroom that is much like the new space between traditional teaching and progressive teaching described by Oyler and Becker (1997)—classroom space that shares both authority and vulnerability. Prep's Parenting classroom is a good example of this.

Discussion-Based Approaches and the Use of Multiple Perspectives

According to Luis, an alumnus, another advantage of Prep's longer and more in-depth classes is that they are—by design—more college-like:

> I like the fact that, you know, the schedule was more college style than anything else. Because we don't . . . like, I know kids that have, you know, 11 periods, you know. And they have 11 different classes, but I felt like, you know, we only had four or five classes a day and everything was so much more concentrated and it prepared you more for college, because you only have, you know, two or three classes a day in college. (interview, March 2007)

A significant number of alumni specifically said that discussion in the classroom prepared them for college and described these discussions as "college-like." For instance, Jenkins, an alumnus, said that he was cognizant of this even as a student at Prep. When asked to describe the classes, he stated:

> I would describe them as kind of what I hoped college would be like. You know, always conversing, always discussing a lot of things, always debating about stuff. And what I did, like, was we never had textbooks, like massive books. It was always, like, sheets of paper. Put it in your binder, you do this sheet, you know, come next day, we'll discuss it, and then you can elaborate on it in class. (interview, March 2007)

Jenkins describes a discussion-based classroom much like the Parenting class. Katerina also pointed out how discussions that transpired at Prep were similar to what she was experiencing at college; she said:

School should be a place where you learn, not just by sitting down and listening to somebody lecturing your classroom, but to actually get involved and be interactive. One thing I remember when I was here is when I was in Amanda's health class and . . . and I will never forget that class because it was so great how we were able to interact. It was like being in college. Now that I am taking health classes in college, I would think back to Amanda's class. Her class just instilled something in me. And I was like yeah, I want to get involved in the sciences. (interview, March 2007)

Shawn, on the other hand, noted that Prep classes were different from some of his college seminars—where he feels less engaged because students are not given as much voice:

It was, like I say, it's much different than a college seminar or college class, because [in those] you'd be lucky if you could get something in to say. I think probably Prep was more college-like than some of these colleges that are here because you're supposed to be able to have a constructive conversation within the lecture. Ideally, the teacher comes in, say . . . she or he has his say for a while, and then everybody discusses the homework or reading from that previous night. I feel a lot of that happened here at Prep. But we weren't only discussing homework, we were discussing what we read during class or, you know, whatever it was at that moment. . . . The classes, because everybody was engaged, they went like that—they went by quick. (interview, May 2007)

Shawn illuminates an interesting phenomenon; he was actually disappointed by his college classes because of what he experienced in discussions at Prep. He was not necessarily critiquing Prep for this incongruity, but rather lamenting not having that level of engagement in college. Shawn was one of several students who described being disappointed with college experiences that were "un-Prep-like" (this phenomenon of disjuncture with the college experience is analyzed in Chapter 8).

Alumni often mentioned that the thematic nature of many classes at Prep was akin to course offerings in college, particularly because, as Alek, alumnus and graduate of a prestigious 4-year university, put it, Prep was "very strong in the esoteric humanities, which helped me in college" (interview, March 2007). Queenia reflected on particular courses that were "college-like":

The classes at Prep were . . . I felt like they were so interesting. It felt to me like being in college. I felt so mature and grown-up and really lucky to be taking the classes that I was, like taking Religion or taking . . . Reconstruction of the South or even the math classes . . . were all so interesting. I felt like the classes were really special at Prep. (interview, May 2007)

Although Queenia includes reference to math classes, almost all of the alumni stated that courses in the social sciences, arts, and humanities at Prep were the ones that prepared them most for college. It was rare to see discussion in math classes, although occasionally this did exist. In most math classes, students generally were clustered in groups of four and engaged in group problem solving. During my fieldwork, there was an emphasis on preparing students for Regents exams and the PBAT, both of which students were expected to complete and pass by the end of sophomore year at that time.[1] This system of dual assessment may have influenced the direction of these classes, although math electives such as Math and Social Justice employed a more hands-on and discussion-based approach.

According to students and alumni, another value of in-depth and thematically structured courses was that they could be tailored to be *culturally responsive* to the student body. For example, Lisa, an alumna of Puerto Rican descent, describes how when she first came to Prep, she was surprised to have a course on Caribbean History. She remembers learning about Pedro Albízu Campos, a Puerto Rican revolutionary:

It was Caribbean History and it was at that point we were talking about Puerto Rico and the U.S. foreign policy issue that was going on. And then we talked about Pedro Albízu Campos and we talked about Luis Munoz Marin. It's funny, I had never heard of Pedro before. I knew Luis . . . I know that his name was familiar, but I didn't exactly know why were these people so prominent in Puerto Rican history and I felt like . . . coming here it was a part of my history. Like, I was learning about myself, so it was interesting. I feel like in another school you don't really have that advantage. So it's pretty . . . I guess . . . more rounded, the education here. (interview, March 2007)

Lisa later explained that this experience "made me want to further learn, like, take it further, like, learn more about the issues that are going on in Puerto Rico," and shared that she was now taking classes at the Institute for Puerto Rican Studies at Hunter College.

In general, students described their classes at Prep as emphasizing deep discussion and using multiple sources to present varied perspectives. Dalia, an alumna, noted:

Whenever I describe the school to people, when they want to know what kind of school I went to, I always describe [Prep] as a liberal arts kind of high school that dealt with teaching, not through textbooks, not through mainstream education, but through actual artifacts, and pieces, and writings. And every single class I took—from art class to music class or history—everything . . . just . . . the depth of it and understanding the topic was what I needed, because I guess maybe I had ADD and didn't know it. But in my other classes [at other schools] even though I would pass and I would do my work, it was a lack of interest, and Prep managed to grab my interest. I guess through different teaching methods. (interview, February 2007)

Dalia describes how pedagogy that emphasizes both depth and multiple perspectives not only engaged her as a student, but made learning interesting—experiences she did not have at other mainstream schools. Other students also noted that discussions brought material to life for them. For example, Lisa remembered classes at Prep as follows:

Definitely different from what I had experienced before coming here because it was all based on lecture. But, the learning was more . . . it was just lecture and sitting in just rows and having the teachers stand there for an hour and just talking. There was no interaction. Like, here in Prep I feel like when we're learning we're also being engaged with the material. We sit in a group and we will discuss the topics. And they encourage us to see what we think about the topics. Basically have a workshop. And I think that's important because honestly I hadn't really learned before coming here. A lot of it is just a blur, but, like, when I came here . . . even now I still remember what I had learned. (interview, March 2007)

Although she had graduated 4 years earlier, Lisa still remembered quite a bit of what she learned. She attributed this to being engaged in the process and being invited to "see what we think," resonating with how students felt that their voices and ideas mattered. This contributed to a discussion-like format where students exchanged ideas and information, and their intellect was respected. According to Sammy, an alumnus, these types of discussions found their way into many different classes and connected to the Core Values, including respect for the intellect:

Well, I mean, in terms of respect to intellect, like, there's a lot of really intellectual stuff going on at Prep. Like, a lot of really good classes with things that might not be discussed in other classes in other schools. And respect to everybody's level of intellect, you know, just something . . . there's something for everybody to feel smart about. (interview, April 2007)

Sammy also notes here that these classes are intellectual and inclusive because "there's something for everybody to feel smart about."

Heterogeneous Groupings

Students and alumni consistently remarked that heterogeneous classroom groupings were a positive aspect of their schooling at Prep. Classes are not only de-tracked by ability level, but also heterogeneously grouped by grade. Students choose their classes based on interest, and together with their advisor, they make sure that the credit the class represents fulfills an aspect of the state requirements for graduation. For instance, a Latin American History class counts toward a Global History credit. This enables students to have a nonsequential curriculum, which is ultimately more college-like in approach and also brings students from different grade levels together. Stacy, a senior, identified her most memorable experience as being a 9th-grader in a mixed-grade class:

> And it's my freshman year . . . there was this one class where I was the only freshman out of a whole bunch of juniors and seniors. And I guess that is what really pushed me to do it, 'cause it was hard . . . [it was] African American Intellectual History. . . . I knew how to push myself in a class around all upperclassmen. So that class really, you know, opened up my eyes to high school itself. (focus group, May 2007)

While math classes at Prep often are separated by grade level because the knowledge tends to be sequential, almost all other classes comprise students from every grade. According to one teacher, Moira, "Being with older students models for younger students how to engage in discussion, and it also raises the maturity level" (interview, March 2007). Many teachers shared this sentiment, acknowledging that the mixed groupings contributed to a more dynamic classroom. This aligns with much of the literature on tracking and de-tracking that examines the effects of both approaches on classroom dynamics and student academic trajectories (Burris & Wellner, 2005; Oakes, 2005; Rubin, 2006).

Moreover, according to the school's founder, Harry, heterogeneous groupings reflect a general commitment to valuing diversity and do not "reproduce some of the worst aspects of traditional schooling through separating kids by grade level" (interview, 2007). Students felt that sharing class time with peers from different grades contributed to a stronger overall sense of community. Joshua, a 9th-grader, commented that this unification strategy is one reason cliques are uncommon in the school:

> I know a lot more people than freshmen, since we have classes with them. I think that's another reason why. We have . . . mixed classes so we know more people. (interview, March 2007)

Like Joshua, many past and current students believed that the mixed grades created more unity among Prep students.

While different rationales may factor into why schools group students in particular ways, students at Prep clearly appreciated the approach at their school. Other schools, like Urban Academy and the James Baldwin School, use similar models that group students across grade levels. Larger schools that have similar missions often have "upper houses" and "lower houses" that might not mix across all four grades, but configure classes between two grades. Shifts from conventional ways of grouping classes can be an intentional strategy that contributes to infusing an HRE approach in the classroom.

External Learning Opportunities

Prep students have many opportunities to take advantage of external partnerships. They can enroll in classes outside of Prep and have various experiences with community partners, which have proved fundamental to their growth and experience and prepared them for postsecondary environments. For instance, Monique, an alumna studying at a private liberal arts college in New England, earned college credit for classes she took as a high school student at the Asia Society—classes that lit the spark of curiosity that led her to pursue Japanese culture as her major. Erin and Shawn similarly received college credit for computer art classes at Eyebeam Atelier and the DIA Center for the Arts. Monique described how formal learning experiences with community partners "allowed me to grow and sort of like to do things I thought I wouldn't do in high school" (interview, March 2007). Erin suggested that these experiences were "just different, refreshing; it was new" (interview, May 2007). Other students described how teachers at Prep often partner with external community groups that add value to their classes, allowing students who do not have time for outside classes to gain exposure to various artistic and community organizations. For example, Luis remembered how his English class partnered with an arts organization called The Kitchen:

> I remember how we went to The Kitchen, and we . . . you know, we were able to see like arts and, you know. Like, that's a lot like . . . a lot of times that's stuff . . . you know, you usually don't get to see, you know, and it definitely helps you to grow as a person. (interview, March 2007)

Luis believes these classroom connections broadened his worldview because "it definitely helps you grow as a person," suggesting that exposure to unexpected resources in the community led to increased academic engagement. Indeed, external connections emphasize a commitment to fostering learning through collaborative community partnerships.

Additionally, students and alumni felt the option to take college classes was an advantage of the Prep curriculum. At the time of this research, Prep had partnerships with The New School and the Borough of Manhattan Community College, where students could take free courses while still enrolled in high school. While they do not get college credit, Prep students have the option to count these classes for a high school requirement. Students described this as an opportunity that broadened their curricular choices and helped prepare them for college. Monique, talking about her classes at the Asia Society, recalled:

> In terms of . . . being able to take college classes outside of Prep . . . it has helped me for how college is like, having to write a paper and having to read a lot. But I guess being able to have that opportunity of how a college classroom is has helped. (interview, March 2007)

Stacey, a current senior who has taken three college classes, remarked in a focus group that this experience was unknown to friends from her neighborhood:

> But like, if it wasn't for Prep, like, most of my friends who go to school in Jamaica [Queens] never took college classes. It's just that, you know, when I compare with my friends that attend other high schools, like, I say, "I go outside for lunch." "You do?" they say. "I call the teachers by their first name." "You do that, too?" And like, certain things I'll be happy or certain privileges . . . that is why I would tell somebody to come here. 'Cause you don't get that elsewhere. But like, the college classes, like I said, most of my friends were like, "College classes—how do you get involved in that?" (May 2007)

While Stacey highlights a few previously discussed characteristics that she believes make Prep unique, she also describes how her friends were particularly impressed that she was able to take college classes. In fact, during my year of fieldwork, 22 students were enrolled in college courses for the spring semester. While most were seniors, this list included some juniors and even one sophomore.

In small schools with fewer offerings than one finds in larger high schools, options for college classes and community partnerships are fundamental to the provision of a broad curriculum and simultaneously reflect the pedagogical principles of an HRE-aligned school. One criticism of small schools is that because they have fewer teachers, they offer fewer courses. Prep resolves that dilemma by augmenting the curriculum with external opportunities for students.

THE CRITICAL AND INTELLECTUAL CLASSROOM: CULTIVATING QUESTIONING, AWARENESS, REFLECTION, AND ACTIVISM

Raising critical consciousness is a fundamental part of both critical pedagogy and human rights education. Many current students and alumni described how the classes and curriculum at Prep either made them aware of things that they were not necessarily aware of before or provided a space in which they could explore complex issues more deeply. At times, students and alumni described a process of gaining self-awareness after becoming engaged by the nature and structure of their classes; however, at other times, they made specific reference to how the curriculum and classes at Prep made them see and make sense of "the world" and their role in it differently. Clearly, content and processes at Prep encourage students to think critically about complex issues and take a stand to advance social change.

A Critical Questioning Lens for Complex Issues

Most classes at Prep are framed around larger essential questions that help students consider a big idea. For instance, one class, the Global Economy and Human Rights, is framed around the central question: Which economic system best maintains and supports human rights for all? Students learn about different economic systems, as well as local and global human rights issues that operate within those economic systems, to ultimately answer the question by the time they leave the class. Another class, the American Dream, uses two central texts—*Invisible Man* by Ralph Ellison and *The Great Gatsby* by F. Scott Fitzgerald, along with supplementary literature— to explore the realities, fictions, and meanings of the American dream.

One pattern I found was that several students described classes that made them interested in and more aware of political movements. For instance, Dalia described the following:

> The one thing I took away with me walking out of that school was they all taught very passionately, and we focused on politics. I loved that they didn't use textbooks; textbooks can get a little bit redundant and I felt that the material that we used . . . one class that always sticks out . . . the class on South Africa. . . . It was actually one of the classes that touched me deeply just because I do identify myself as an African, so to be able to learn about different parts of that huge continent, everything that went on there. I remember when we got to South Africa and we started talking about Apartheid, I vividly remember being a young child—like 4, 5, or 6 even—it was the fall of Apartheid and it was constant news coverage, media, all you saw on television, and songs were being sung about Mandela on the streets. . . . To learn about that years down the line and reconnect with that moment was phenomenal, maybe that's why it still sticks out. Also, another thing about education, if you will, you see a lot of students—a lot of people actually, even adults—who might not know about a different era, a different time period, whether it be through fashion, music, politics . . . and so to, I guess kind of be

educated through school about those different aspects was, you know, phenomenal. (interview, February 2007)

In this passage, Dalia describes learning more about something she was vaguely familiar with in her childhood. Explaining that to "years down the line . . . reconnect with that moment was phenomenal," she talks about expanding upon something relevant to her own life and childhood experience, and ultimately feeling better informed. Similarly, Erin, an alumna, discussed "political" discussions at Prep:

> I liked the fact that Prep was open-minded . . . when you take college classes, everybody's really political and everybody's really opinionated and that reminded me a lot of the teachers and classes at Prep, because they didn't have a problem talking about Communism and what they really thought about Communism. . . . That's what I really liked. You could really talk about serious stuff . . . not to the extent where it's disrespectful, but to the extent that you could share your opinions and talk about something important. You don't get that a lot. (interview, May 2007)

Erin notes that in political discussion, students at Prep were invited to share their opinions about "serious stuff" in a respectful way. This demonstrates how the culture of respect among students and teachers translated into the academic arena.

Yet, according to Queenia, learning about politics was not simply about content; politics was a topical platform for a way of thinking and analyzing that normalized critical questioning. She explained, "I think I learned to be . . . definitely I learned to be interested in politics. I learned to definitely question things more, definitely to analyze things more" (interview, May 2007). Many students and alumni described a similar phenomenon. Giancarlo, an 11th-grader, stated, "It's like you gotta think beyond thinking" (interview, May 2007). One alumnus, Alek, said, "This might come off poorly, but I don't think I learned all that much at Prep. More importantly though, I learned *how* to learn and think at Prep" (interview, March 2007). As someone who came to Prep with advanced math and reading skills, Alek may have felt that he had already developed skills in these areas. Nonetheless, while his statement may come off as critical at first, Alek makes the point that he learned analytical skills that may be more valuable to him than actual content, as these ways of thinking provided him with a lens that will help him make sense of his life in the long term.

Indeed, another pattern that emerged from the data was that many students stated explicitly that they believe Prep is unique in its approach to thinking and analysis. For example, when asked whether he would recommend the school to others, Sammy, an alumnus who had been a transfer student from a prestigious public high school, stated:

> I'd tell him . . . well, I guess I'd ask him would you want to be at a school that you can just totally, like, immerse yourself in, like, every single club and sports activity and AP classes and stuff like that . . . like going to huge big school events, games, I wouldn't suggest going to Prep. Like probably just go to [previous school] type school because that's the kind of school that that would be. . . . But if you're not exactly sure what it is that you want to be doing in high school, if you go to class and . . . you kind of wonder what you're doing there sometimes, then I think Prep is a good place because they let you do more of what it is that you want to do, while still learning a lot. (interview, April 2007)

While Sammy is not overly critical of his previous school and realizes it is a good option for certain students, he distinguishes Prep as a more appropriate place to ask larger existential questions with less one-size-fits-all learning.

Students and alumni often attribute Prep's push toward analytical thinking to the fact that teachers do not rely on one source, textbook, or program geared toward tests to guide the class. In a focus group, Diana, an 11th-grader who had been at Prep since 9th grade, stated:

> Our school's different because we don't take a lot of tests. And, like, if you compare other schools, they . . . teach from, like, books. Like, if they give you books, the teachers would teach from it and that's the only thing you can learn. And . . . when you come to Prep, you might come with a closed mind and come out with an open mind because you interact with your teachers more. And you learn about different things that happened in the world. And, like, sometimes, students . . . ask questions that lead the class. And it's more, like, students lead than teachers sometimes. (May 2007)

Diana describes her schooling experience and environment as one that is transformative, and her description mirrors some of the processes described in critical pedagogy. Moreover, she talks about interacting with teachers more and how students sometimes lead the direction of the class. In this sense, Diana is not only acknowledging a validation of student knowledge, she is also describing some of the aspects of the intergenerational community that have been described by other students.

Some alumni described the push toward thinking critically as something that helped them in college. For example, Luis, when describing the teachers at Prep, recalled that in class they encouraged him to ask questions and think, something he found useful in college:

Oh the teachers are excellent. You know, the teachers, they encouraged me to think . . . to use my brain and to not to take anything at face value; to really ask questions and ask ultimately why? . . . And that sort of free-thinking helps in college, especially when a teacher . . . when they're teaching and it's a lecture class and there's not a lot of talking from the students. If the teacher's just sitting there, you know, reading from a book, you don't have any fear to just raise your hand and say, why is that? Or why is this? You know, and it helps you learn to get more out of the . . . out of the text. They [the classes at Prep] were interesting. You know, when I was in class, I was interested in learning. You know, everything, like I said, the teachers encouraged questions and encouraged growth. So, I was happy that I was able to speak and that there was more discussion than lecture. (interview, March 2007)

Luis describes how the normalization of thinking critically and questioning helped him not only feel comfortable in college, but also "get more out of the text" and grow intellectually. This overlaps with the previous discussion in this chapter regarding how students value the type of discourse and atmosphere that makes Prep classes "college-like."

Overall, students and alumni expressed that the type of education enacted at Prep allowed them to learn more about the world through the lens of critical questioning. The following three excerpts [emphasis added] share remarkably similar language about this process:

[On what she liked most about the school] I loved being asked what I thought about things. I loved having the chance to talk to people. I loved being able to have intellectual conversations with people and I loved being able to come together as a community, the whole school, and discuss and talk and relate and get to know each other. I loved that I was encouraged to *take a look at the world* around me. I loved that. (Queenia, alumna, interview, May 2007)

[On what she learned most at Prep] I guess to believe in myself more. Also, *I learned about issues in the world* that I wasn't even aware of until I came here because at my other school we didn't really talk about that. It was all just from the book stuff. (Lisa, alumna, interview, March 2007)

[On what she likes most about the school] Well, the discussions we would have in class. And most . . . discussions and the lessons that the teachers would give us . . . it's just *exposing us to . . . the problems and issues . . . going on in the world.* (Magdalena, 12th-grader, interview, March 2007)

While it is standard for any NY State high school to teach "about the world" through the Regents-based global studies curriculum, these students describe this process as if it were unique. Queenia links it to an overall sense of community, Lisa frames it in terms of issues that are not discussed in her old school, and Magdalena suggests that a critical lens and exposure to complex problems are ways Prep students examine world issues. At the time she was interviewed, Magdalena was taking a Global Economics and Human Rights class. She talked about preparing for an in-depth class "re-negotiation" of the NAFTA treaty. Students had different roles that supported various positions along the spectrum of opinion regarding NAFTA. Magdalena's comment may have been rooted in the fact that discussing these multiple perspectives was allowing her to explore many of the complexities of free trade; she was playing the role of a factory worker in Detroit.[2]

Victor, a 12th-grade transfer student, brought up how differently complex topics had been approached in his previous public high school:

> I learned about globalization. Everybody learns about it. Like I said, I learned about globalization when I was a freshman in my old school, but the way this teacher at Prep taught it, taught me a different way. I guess I learned the basics of why the world is the way it is, like the series of events that took place that made it happen that way. . . . At my old school, I had only one teacher at my old school like that. Even he used to try to teach us . . . we used to read the textbook in class, but every time we used to read a chapter, he used to try to tell us the other side of the story. He was a traveling teacher. His name was Mr. E. But he's the only good teacher I had in the old school. (interview, May 2007)

Victor does not negate that there might be possibilities for a critical approach to making sense of the world in other schools, but his description insinuates that he believes it is a fundamental feature of Prep, whereas at his old school he just happened to have been lucky enough, by chance, to learn from one critically minded teacher.

Project-Based Assessment

Alumni highlighted additional ways Prep had prepared them for the critical thinking they needed in college. Although students had to take Regents exams in math and English language arts for several years, Prep always maintained a strong focus on and commitment to project-based assessment and feedback. Many students commented that the performance-based assessment tasks (PBATs), described briefly in Chapter 1, helped them prepare for the rigors of writing papers in college. For example, Luis, an alumnus who started at Hofstra University but transferred to Hunter College for financial reasons, commented that the writing and the feedback he received from doing a PBAT prepared him more than a Regents exam:

> When I first came here I thought, PBATs were a ridiculous idea and because I thought . . . I mean, I'm a good test-taker, so I thought it would be better for me to take the Regents, but eventually, you know, as I went to the whole feedback process, I felt like that . . . people that's helped me understand, more than, you know, if I was to just sit there and take a test. You know, and I remember when I was taking the SAT, I was like, I wish I could do another feedback, because, when you study for the SATs just, you know, you're just trying to memorize stuff and then you forget it afterwards, but the stuff that I remember from my feedback . . . I take it with me wherever I go. . . . [For science PBAT] I had an actual . . . an experiment with them with ampicillin and bacteria, which was great. I did that with Nayara [science teacher]. I also had different essays that I had in my history class that I had to revise . . . it was great because, you know, it actually helped me write and helped me make that essay professional. I've taken that skill with me to college because in college, you have to be very specific and, you know, where'd you get this source from? . . . So all that feedback, you know, it helped me more for college than, you know . . . a Regents could. (interview, March 2007)

Luis not only describes a process that he believes prepared him for college, but describes it in a way that shows he was actively engaged in his learning. He compares this with taking a standardized test where the process was memorization "to just sit there and take a test."

Infusing Activism

Some students and alumni suggested that beyond an impetus to think critically about the world, there was also a push for members of the Prep community to work actively toward social change and activism. For instance, Rebecca, an alumna, recalled:

> I remember us with pickets, "we don't want the Regents; we don't want the Regents." I remember in Alex's class going outside and naming the trees on the street, like who does that in high school? Naming a tree, what? As Prep students, as a Prep community we are aware of the things around us, and we try to fight to make the positive things stay and the negative things go away fast. (interview, January 2007)

In this passage, Rebecca describes what she believes to be a fundamental value of the school: "to fight to make the positive things stay and the negative things go away fast." She notes that this was integrated specifically into class content. For instance, the Community Action class at Prep, which counts for Participation in Government credit, not only places students with community activist organizations for an internship, but also requires them to engage in an activist project that addresses an issue in the school. The types of projects are wide-ranging and include school beautification projects, workshops on LGBTQIA issues for students, fundraising as a school for a specific cause such as the AIDS Walk, and so on. Projects are self-determined by the students in small team groupings.

Sometimes students would feel empowered by the knowledge and skills they gained from their classes and think of ways to bring that information or experience to the larger student body. While Advisory was a space in which students often did this, classes also gave students room to translate their skills into action. For instance, students in the Caribbean History class gave workshops at the end of the semester for the rest of the school in three separate "Quads" (mini-Town Meetings that consist of four advisories together). One group focused their Quad on a discussion about the environmental impact of the U.S. Navy presence on the island of Vieques in Puerto Rico, even after the Navy technically left; another group ran a discussion about the U.S. embargo on Cuba and its implications for Cubans; a third group focused on lingering colonial and imperial effects on political violence in Haiti and considered whether U.S. immigration laws should be changed to grant Haitian refugees the same rights as Cuban refugees. In these sessions, students were not only sharing particular content and knowledge with their peers, but engaging them with the same type of critical questioning and push toward social change that they had been part of in the class.

Overall, the theme of activism, which will be analyzed in greater detail in Chapter 7, is thoughtfully integrated into many classes at the school. While educational policy reform has focused primarily on reducing achievement gaps in math and reading, these policies have failed to address other important goals related to critical thinking and problem solving (Rothstein, Jacobsen, & Wilder, 2008). Those who participated in this research definitely voiced how beneficial and long-lasting critical thinking and problem-solving skills are.

NAVIGATING POSTSECONDARY MATH CURRICULA: CONSIDERATIONS

As described earlier in this chapter, most Prep alumni felt well prepared to engage in postsecondary discussion-based seminars because of Prep's emphasis on writing and in-class discussions. However, there also seemed to be a feeling among several alumni that Prep's math program did not prepare them for postsecondary environments as well as the school's programs in the humanities and social sciences. For example, when asked about what needs to change at Prep, Luis responded:

Well, I mean . . . I don't know if they changed the curriculum, but I didn't feel like the math part prepared me so much for college. You know, because I had to take a remedial class. As far as English is concerned that was, you know, excellent and like college. I was very happy with my time at Prep, especially when you had to do the intensives and stuff like that, and everything else. But I think the math left a little . . . you know, a little to be desired. (interview, March 2007)

Luis's response conveys an almost hesitant tone, as if this criticism, which is incisive in its indictment of the math program, may jeopardize other aspects of the school curriculum. Nonetheless, similar critiques emerged repeatedly among alumni. Alek, an alumnus who graduated from an elite private university, felt that his skills in math had stagnated at Prep:

Prep was fantastic at the liberal arts education but I lost any and all proficiency I had in math, which I was doing well in, up to that point. Not all that shocking considering the name of the school, but still. I feel like that part of my academic potential was lost, but that's really not Prep's fault nor do I know if I would've pursued that, used that, been better off, etc. The biggest measure is am I happy with my life? Yes. Did Prep help me get there? Yes. (interview, March 2007)

Like Luis, Alek emphasizes that other aspects of Prep were "fantastic" and even contributed to his subsequent happiness. He goes on to say that losing his academic potential in math is "really not Prep's fault." Perhaps these students critique the math program in apologetic ways because they do not want the school to change and risk losing some of the other important characteristics that make it unique. Despite this, alumni repeatedly suggested that they were not quite prepared for the rigors of college math. In fact, at Prep Alumni Day during the period of my fieldwork, alumni met with staff at their weekly meeting and resoundingly suggested that the math program should be more rigorous to better prepare students for the challenges of college math (fieldnotes, January 11, 2007).

It should be noted that, according to the two math teachers interviewed for this study, Alek was unlike most students at Prep. Both math teachers talked about how most students have "math phobia" coming into the school, so one of the main goals, according to Marcel, a math teacher, "is to make them comfortable and feel like they can do math" (interview, March 2007). Interestingly, none of the current students interviewed complained about the math program, and many mentioned that for the first time, they actually liked math. For example, Richie stated:

Before I got here I hated math, but then as years kept going, I became an honors math student. I'm pretty good in math now. So, I have a bright future now, 'cause I want to go to school for business and in order to go to school for business you got to know math and your numbers and stuff like that, so I should do good in the future. (focus group, May 2007)

Richie's example echoed the feedback of many current students. One alumnus, Jenkins, also mentioned that he overcame his math aversion while at Prep:

> I didn't like math, and I still don't particularly like math, but I had a lot of math teachers who had my back and helped me with mathematics, so I didn't hate it as much. I kind of hug it from now on. (interview, March 2007)

By stating that he now "kind of hugs it," Jenkins suggests that he has become more open and confident toward the subject. Jenkins had deferred college admission for a year to work, so he had yet to take college math. Nonetheless, the excerpts related to math at Prep reveal an interesting paradox. On the surface, they may seem to suggest that academic rigor in math was sacrificed so students could feel comfortable and confident enough to pass their PBAT and graduate. However, further investigation poses much more complex issues. Math teachers reported grappling with the overall low math skills of most (not all) students entering Prep and having to deal with basic remediation on that (entry) level. While Prep students eventually completed their high school math requirement and most went on to college, they often struggled there because their mathematical skills were insufficient.

This tension surfaces some deeper and important questions about the potential "academic costs" of constructivist, student-centered programs, particularly as math attainment and access to STEM careers remain issues of equity and social justice for those most marginalized from these professions and trajectories. While many advocates of standards-based reform would say that it indeed comes at high cost, most past and current Prep students present more variegated accounts of their experiences and might address this dilemma differently. What directions and strategies might allow schools and teachers to proactively address issues and tensions related to preparing students for *all* facets of postsecondary work and schooling—without sacrificing the constructivist nature of their programs?

Prep, for example, has made significant changes to more explicitly address the comparative weakness of the math curriculum by implementing concrete strategies to bridge HRE and math education. The math program was switched from an entirely constructivist approach (IMP Math) to a combination approach (CMP Math), which appears to be more suitable for students who do not have high foundational levels of numeracy when they enter Prep. Teachers have begun to work across disciplines to find ways to infuse math skills in other areas; for instance, there is an effort to use statistics and math skills in history classes to help students understand certain historical phenomena.

Schools like Prep also can advise graduating students about which postsecondary environments tend to employ approaches to the math curriculum that might be more familiar. For instance, Tyner-Mullings (2012) shows that while Central Park East Secondary School (CPESS) students may have felt underprepared for entry-level survey math classes at institutions like CUNY and SUNY, students could engage in upper-level, applied, and in-depth math courses at those same institutions because of the type of work they had done at CPESS. In fact, Amelia, a former Prep student, said that while attending graduate school at the University of Chicago, she was far better prepared than her peers for her statistics class because of the math classes she had in high school at Prep (interview, 2012).

It is also important to note that at the time of my ethnographic research, Prep had to administer the Regents exam in mathematics, as the state waiver did not extend to that subject at that time. Thus, students were taking the math Regents exam like other students in the state, as well as working on their math PBATs. I point this out because by no means does this study suggest that a Regents-based math curriculum will prepare students for the math rigors of college. Moreover, data on de-tracked and nonhierarchical math classrooms have shown that these classrooms worked toward equity more effectively than those that are tracked (Boaler, 2006; Burris, Heubert, & Levin, 2006; I. S. Horn, 2006; Walker, 2012). Thus, simply turning back to tracked and traditional classrooms may not necessarily address what seems to be a largely systemic issue, and that strategy also might exacerbate unequal opportunities and inequity in general.

CONCLUSION: THE CASE FOR CRITICAL QUESTIONING IN SCHOOLS

Overall, Prep students' nuanced accounts of their schooling experiences give us an opportunity to consider how important it is for high school students to experience a school culture characterized by critical questioning and a system of schooling that views and treats them as intellectually capable young people. Participants in this study enthusiastically described an academic environment that encouraged them to enjoy learning and embrace intellectualism, and also challenged them to analyze and think about the world in ways that had been absent in their previous mainstream standards-based schooling environments. Students, both current and former, articulated that these approaches helped them find real purpose in school, contributed to their academic engagement, impacted their outlook on the world, and gave them the sense that they should get involved in improving their community and in social change. Moreover, they specifically spoke of how they have benefitted—even in the long term—from the transfer of "nonacademic" skills that strengthened their abilities to problem solve, actively engage in social change initiatives, practice tolerance, and value true diversity. While several former students were concerned about the quality of Prep's math program, this chapter ultimately shows that it was the in-depth, project- and discussion-based classes that former and current students most remembered and appreciated about Prep, and that these classes benefited and prepared them for postsecondary life. Looking specifically at an aspect of Prep's curriculum that was perceived as being comparatively weak highlighted an instance of how schools might incorporate critical feedback and adapt their practices to assuage some of the tensions and imbalances that can arise in participatory learning environments.

CHAPTER 7

The Components of Participation

Schooling That Fosters Democracy and Student Agency

There were ups and downs but we had freedom to express that as students and boy, oh boy, those Town Meetings, true democracy, who could ever forget those? Classic forums that stood out from many other high schools. Period. I often look back and think about the good old Prep days and realize how crucial to my life and important they were, especially when I look at the chaos in many school systems today as a Teacher's Assistant and see how administration and politics cheat the system while students get the short end of the stick. I think man was blessed to come across Humanities Prep. (Khaleel, alumnus, survey, 2007)

This chapter highlights the importance of participatory spaces in school life, another major strategy to make human dignity a pivotal aspect of school reform. While I showed previously that Prep academically engages young people by institutionalizing strong student–teacher relationships; a Core Values–infused culture of respect; and a thematic, culturally relevant, and project-based curriculum, this chapter focuses on a complementary strategy that makes Prep unusual—its efforts to engage students as participatory actors in the school environment through nonacademic structures. The importance of such an approach in the development of the students' lives is not to be underestimated, as Khaleel, an alumnus, remarked in the survey. The participation component contributes to a culture of critical consciousness and agency, a culture that is fundamental and necessary to institutionalize an HRE framework in schools.

My research suggests that enacting this type of education in public school settings results in very promising outcomes when school structures are designed to support its dissemination. Overwhelmingly, the students, teachers, and alumni with whom I spoke described distinctive, nonacademic participatory spaces and practices at Prep that provide room for transformative agency, allow students to cultivate their "voice" and explore new ways of thinking about complex issues and their role in the world, and challenge students to use active approaches to advance individual and structural change. Based on these findings, I assert that Advisory, Town Meetings/Quads, and the Fairness Committee—coupled with the comprehensive, thematic, inquiry-based curriculum described in the previous chapter—are participatory aspects of school life at Prep. They help (re)socialize students academically by fostering critical participation and providing various opportunities for students to build effective communication skills, question what is presented to them as truth, work through disagreements, confront complexity, and imagine different alternatives for the future.

While it is impossible to gauge whether schools can be wholly transformative, students and alumni consistently attributed various successes in their lives to skills they developed in Prep's intentional nonacademic spaces for democratic engagement. The fact that Prep students and alumni consistently link their own academic, social, and emotional well-being to specific participatory schooling experiences reflects both the practices and the goals of HRE, underscoring the importance of including participatory practices in school reform. The following sections will highlight the three participatory structures that students and alumni consistently mentioned as having the biggest effect on their schooling experience at Prep.

ADVISORY

Advisory, a daily class period of 15 students, is a time for students to discuss issues relevant to their lives, receive academic support, develop leadership skills, and build community with other members of their Advisory group. "[Advisory is where] people can make themselves be heard . . . in a smaller setting where it can be a little bit more private" (Sammy, alumnus, interview, April 28, 2007). Every teacher is assigned to one Advisory. On a typical day, one can walk into an Advisory and see a workshop on college readiness; in another, a heated discussion about the salaries of female athletes; in yet another, an exploration of the causes of domestic violence. These are issues that stem from students' own interests, and students often are asked to come up with topics for discussion and debate.

Former and current students resoundingly described Advisory as a setting that fosters more participatory engagement, and further described it as being essential to students' academic, social, and emotional well-being in school. While Advisory is not an academic class, Advisories provide a consistent space in the school for students to check in with their teacher/advisor and peers about schoolwork, personal issues, and concerns. Erin describes it as a place to breathe in a frantic school day: "I think I love the fact that you guys had an Advisory system. I think that's just better 'cause I think that it was too hectic and too . . . everybody was so frantic about getting their work done" (interview, May 18, 2007). According to the former and founding principal, Advisory is one of the structures in the school that helps students navigate both external and internal pressures because it provides a "decent amount of guidance" and programmatically provides "an adult who cares" (interview, March 19, 2007). He explains Advisory as a setting where "the *students* are the curriculum" (interview, June 15, 2007).

All teachers at Prep are expected to run an Advisory group, although new teachers often are paired with seasoned teachers to have experienced support in implementing this "nonacademic" curriculum. Teachers agree that Advisory at Prep is very valuable, particularly as many other schools implement this strategy but use it more as a brief homeroom experience than as a strategic, small-scale, participatory learning community. According to Adrian, a teacher who taught at a few other schools with Advisory programs in place, "A lot of schools pay lip service to the idea [of Advisory]. Prep really invests quite a lot of time in what most would term a nonacademic but credit-bearing class. . . . I mean I think Prep puts its money where its mouth is around Advisory, at least in setting aside time for it" (interview, May 8, 2007).

My own experience working with student teachers in other small schools with Advisory programs confirms Adrian's comment. In most schools I have visited where Advisory meets once a week, students usually talk among themselves or do homework and there is little sense of communal or larger conversation. In contrast, Prep teachers and students generally use this daily time to talk about school and personal issues as a group, and teachers often use those topics of conversation as a way to establish linkages to issues in society at large.

In many ways, Advisory is seen as a formalized place to solidify close relationships among students and advisors/teachers in the ways described in Chapter 4. While this does not preclude students from going to other teachers with whom they have strong relationships, students know that Advisory—and the role of the advisor—carries with it particular expectations. Kevin, an alumnus, spoke of regularly seeking out his advisor because she "was open to me" and "provided me with excellent advice and pushed me in a positive direction" (interview, December 20, 2007). Katerina, an alumna, similarly describes her advisor as someone who provided almost unconditional support: "She was very inspirational for me because she was my advisor my second semester and senior year. She made me feel very confident that even though I did badly in the past I can still go on and do a lot better" (interview, March 22, 2007).

These themes of care and support echo the ways students viewed many of their teachers, as highlighted in Chapter 4. Formal structures like Advisory ensure that students have a strong relationship with at least one teacher, their advisor. While all teachers are expected to be friendly to and know the students, the advisor role is much closer to formal mentorship. For instance, Deena described her advisor as "nosy, compassionate, because I wasn't showing up to school and I really, really appreciate that, because it showed that she really cared. She was a very compassionate human being. It showed that she really cared about her students" (interview, December 20, 2006).

While some teachers tended to reach out to students who were not advisees, there is an explicit expectation at Prep that the advisor will serve as an active person in the advisee's life. This seems to work well; Prep students feel that their advisors can help them with specific problems because the advisors know them so well. For instance, Victor explained, "I go to her because she's my advisor and because her outlook on things is, like, analytical, and it helps me think about, like, how to . . . it's like problem solving. So she helps me solve problems" (interview, May 2007). Again, the advisor/advisee relationship does not prevent students from building personal relationships with other teachers, but since there is an expected relationship with a particular advisor, students often rely on that person for guidance.

Interestingly, students also seek out other student members of their Advisory group to get support and guidance from them. Robin, a recent transfer, explained:

> I would want my kids to go [to Prep]. I would really start a school like this; if they tried to close this school down. . . . Because I think that it helps a lot of people that don't have confidence in themselves; like, that don't think that they can make it. It helps them open up . . . and a lot of other schools; they don't teach students that. . . . Like, the fact that we have advisors . . . like, I never went to a school with an advisor . . . it's not exactly one-on-one but if you have a problem, you could always pull your advisor to the side and tell her what you're going through. I think that affects a lot of people because a lot of people don't have people to talk to at home. Like, people are in different situations; so it's good when you're able to come to school and really release the things that you're going through. Like, it makes people feel good about themselves. So, I would definitely recommend people to come to this school. (interview, May 11, 2007)

While Robin mentions that she can pull aside her advisor at any point, she also acknowledges that it is not always "one-on-one." By stating this, she recognizes that there is a whole community of support within her Advisory, though she acknowledges the key role her advisor plays.

Marcel, a math teacher and advisor, explained that Advisory helps the school community realize the mission of the school. He noted, "You can get these kids to listen to each other and really try to relate . . . you've got people from very different backgrounds and you're trying to get them to understand each other's situations" (interview, March 14, 2007). Thus, Advisory not only solidifies relationships among students and their teachers, it is also a time and place to build a smaller community within the larger one, develop ideas, and cultivate student voice in a more intimate setting. Mark, a teacher, shared, "Advisory is a structure that most allows for the fostering of democracy" (interview, June 12, 2006). During Advisory, Mark often used "go around" techniques to engage all students as speakers and also allow them to assume leadership of the topics and discussions. During one observation, a student, Marcus, led an Advisory on the topic of "Interracial Relationships," because it interested him. After explaining his own experience as the child of an interracial relationship, he asked the other students, "Do you think they can work?" At that point, each student in the room gave a brief response, and then they segued into a larger conversation about institutionalized racism, moving beyond the personal and analyzing the topic from a systemic perspective. This demonstrates how relevant, student-led discussions transpire democratically in Advisory—discussions that may not have room to exist in a more formally "academic" setting. Further, these participatory experiences prepare students to engage in the larger participatory formats that exist in the school.

TOWN MEETINGS/QUADS

Town Meetings/Quads are the second structure students referenced as an integral participatory space at Prep.[1] As weekly whole-school gatherings where students and teachers discuss issues ranging from personal to global, Town Meetings/Quads often expand upon themes explored in Advisory, encouraging further debate and questioning. Each Advisory rotates leadership of Town Meetings/Quads, allowing for a range of perspectives and issues, as well as facilitation styles. Topics for discussion vary and include issues such as school policies, police brutality, political prisoners, and military recruitment in schools. Guest speakers often are invited to come to Town Meetings/Quads. For instance, a guest speaker from a local organization once joined a discussion about environmental racism; another time, a former Black Panther came to discuss and compare activism in the 1970s with activism today. Guests are also invited to address issues of peace, war, and militarism. For instance, in the years leading to the U.S. war and occupations of Afghanistan and Iraq, there were several panels on this topic (see Hantzopoulos, 2004). Moreover, topics in Town Meeting or Quad are philosophical as well.

The following excerpt from my fieldnotes describes, briefly, what might happen in a Quad:

> Clarissa's Quad was doing an activity called "Random Topic." In this Quad, the students leading it actually pretended that they were all talking about their own thing. This was an intentional ploy before uncovering the main topic. Charlie started it off with a spoken word piece.

Then, several joined in. Hawthorne started talking about an "invisible man that robs the bank." Robin talked about the most successful person she knows about. Clarissa and Sebastien went on to talk about the mayor. Britta talked about her favorite pet. Mikaela spoke about "what makes my day." Hawthorne interrupted her and it almost escalated into a fight. At this point, everyone realized that the whole thing was an act. This segued into a larger discussion, "Do students have freedom of speech?" Students and teachers had many different things to say on the subject, and their opinions ranged. Loretta kept the speakers list the whole time and managed the different voices. Students and teachers went on to have a nuanced and layered discussion about what constitutes free speech and when they have it, and also made larger connections to consumerism and capitalism. The conversation kept shifting, but ultimately ended in a broader discussion around whether (or not) wealth or grassroots movements are the catalysts for change. (January 13, 2007)

In this "typical" Quad, an Advisory planned an agenda around an issue to stimulate conversation, in this case, the issue of freedom of speech, although connections were made to consumerism and capitalism. There was then extensive dialogue and exchange of ideas among the students, although no resolution or solution to the problem emerged. Even the principal chimed in; he brought up the point that freedom of speech is a "double-edged sword" and described how this paradox manifests when you can harm someone by what you say. This was a process of students and teachers collectively grappling with ideas together in this space.

Quads/Town Meetings are planned mostly by students in the Advisory whose turn it is to lead with the topic of their choice; thus, these spaces privilege students' perspectives not only in the actual meeting, but also in the preparation of the agenda. In fact, it is not uncommon to see students going from Advisory to Advisory to poll other students about topics a few days before a Town Meeting/Quad. This activity indicates that while members of one particular Advisory have control of the agenda during their week, those in control are interested in creating something that also reflects other students' input. This illustrates one way that students interact democratically among themselves.

According to Nick, a social worker at Prep, these types of forums are a necessary structure in the school because they encourage students to form their own ideas and discuss them with others. He commented:

I was just in a Quad not too long ago and the issue was "nonacademic" but it brought up some very . . . kids just went to a personal place and felt comfortable articulating what they thought and felt in a very large group and I was just struck at how unusual I think that is among teenagers. So to then sit in a college classroom and feel comfortable enough to express your thought, whether it be material or personal, is, I think, important. (interview, March 14, 2007)

In Nick's view, these forums help students feel comfortable sharing their ideas, so that, presumably, students will feel more confident sharing their opinions in college. During my fieldwork, staff generally felt that Town Meetings/ Quads were spaces in which students could be heard on issues that were local, personal, school-specific, and global. Staff more or less expressed that this was a place to ensure that democracy was upheld in the school.

Alumni and students felt very positive about Town Meetings/Quads when they reflected on this structure. In interviews, participants repeatedly said that Town Meetings/Quads were a particular structure in the school that allowed them to develop and share their voices. For instance, Sandra, a senior at the time, explained:

[We] have things like Town Meetings and Quads . . . we get to speak on the topic that we choose, any topic that we like to talk about, and . . . it makes you want to speak about it. And, I feel that before I was never around that kind of environment, that kind of school where . . . we can speak freely. So, I feel that this school has made my voice a bit stronger and I feel that this school makes education more fun, you know, I feel that it's not that textbook-based kind of learning, it's all kinds of learning. (focus group, May 18, 2007)

Town Meetings/Quads, as Sandra suggests, are spaces that allow for the validation of student knowledge, as well as space for contestation. Similarly, Sammy, an alumnus, talked about how Town Meetings allowed him to "be himself," showing how the space formalized some of the processes and attitudes described earlier:

And, you know, Town Meeting . . . if you had something to say about the school, you know, you could say it in front of the whole school and everybody would hear it. So, you know, people weren't afraid to say what was on their mind. I think it was just a really good atmosphere and environment for people to, like I said, just to be themselves genuinely, instead of at another place, where you might try to fit into certain roles. (interview, April 28, 2007)

For some, like Katerina, this translated into being able to develop skills beyond the sphere of schooling:

[At] Prep I was able to speak how I felt. And [Town Meetings] . . . were very inspiring. We were taught how to get up and speak in front of a group or community. When I was at my former high school or even when I was in junior high they didn't teach us that. (interview, March 22, 2007)

In addition to contrasting this experience and opportunity with her previous schooling, Katerina stated that this influenced her current activism as a Doula (an advocate for women giving birth): "It was easier for me to organize other Doulas because I was comfortable speaking in front of large crowds, like we did at Prep" (interview, March 22, 2007). Erin, another alumna, echoed this sentiment and also explained how she learned at Prep to listen attentively to others, "during Town Meetings . . . everybody had to be respectful to everybody's words. It was really hard to not disrespect anybody because everybody believed in something differently" (interview, March 18, 2007). In this sense, Town Meetings/Quads are another way to institutionalize the diffusion and assimilation of a school's core values and foster a community of respectful engagement.

Students often express frustration at Town Meetings, but many suggested that disagreements are necessary for student growth. Because the topics of debate often conjure varied perspectives among students and staff, students frequently feel irritated immediately after a Town Meeting. Amelia stated, "I would keep Town Meetings. Even though they annoyed me when I was at Prep . . . I really do think they keep the community better, I really do" (interview, March 11, 2007). Kevin agreed that while he was challenged in these forums, Town Meetings "gave me a chance to explore ideas and my own pursuits and pushed me to be more open-minded to others' ideas and, well, the world" (interview, December 20, 2007). For Monique, an alumna, it was a new experience to be "seeing environments where people do talk about issues, really" (interview, March 20, 2007).

Town Meetings, therefore, are forums that enable students to make connections between their lives and the world. Lisa, an alumna, explained that this led to awareness of global concerns: "That was our time to talk about issues that were going on in the world or current events. And I feel it's important to come together as a school and actually have that time to talk about issues like that . . . to keep the kids alert of what's going on and also get their views" (interview, March 27, 2007). Dalia, another alumna, explicitly connected these discussions to "critical thinking":

I remember Town Meeting . . . I mean they literally got the whole school together and they would pick up a topic to talk about, whatever was hot at the time . . . it opened up your eyes and your ears to a lot of people's opinions. But, it was a good way to enhance your critical thinking and it embodied how every human should be . . . consider themselves one entity as opposed to different races who don't communicate with each other. (interview, February 15, 2007)

Collectively, these students explain how Town Meetings/Quads build community by engaging multiple perspectives and situating diverse outlooks as a predictable and acceptable phenomenon. According to Fine et al. (1997), schools must not only create desegregated spaces in order to deal with differences among students, but also interrupt institutionally produced identities to nurture multiracial and multiethnic communities. Structures like Town Meetings/Quads allow students and teachers to work toward "creating spaces where differences are acknowledged and respected" (Fine et al., 1997, p. 247).

Town Meetings/Quads also led some students to see how they could become involved in activities beyond the school. Specifically, several participants mentioned that large community forums would help address issues and concerns in their neighborhoods. For example, Rebecca, an alumna, suggested that community forums might help people become "more involved" in the community where she grew up. Ana, a 9th-grader, suggested that she would handle the lack of youth activities in her neighborhood in a way that paralleled some aspects of Town Meetings: "I would, like, hold a big meeting and do some things like sports or something like that so we could get reacquainted" (interview, March 6, 2007). While they do not mention Town Meetings/Quads as a catalyst for organizing community meetings, these students' words do perhaps reveal that they believe these types of forums can create among participants a sense of hope, community involvement, and responsibility for change.

It is important to note that Prep lost its Town Meeting room right before my official fieldwork started. When the school was forced to move to a new space in 2005, staff designated a large room for Town Meetings and converted a smaller room for Prep Central. After realizing that the cramped Prep Central room was not conducive to the types of activities that generally transpired in that space, staff and students moved Prep Central to the Town Meeting room. As a result, Town Meetings thereafter were held in the auditorium or in the library. Neither of these rooms was on the second floor of the building where Prep was located, and they were not always available when the school needed them. Moreover, the set-up of these rooms made it difficult to conduct the forums.

The space issue may seem minor, but the lack of a suitable, convenient space for Town Meetings/Quads has a potentially tremendous effect on a school's ability to fully realize a mission to engage students. The importance of Town Meetings in the development of Prep students' lives is not to be underestimated, as reflected in many of the remarks I included in this section. Without an appropriate space for Town Meetings, the "true democracy" described by Khaleel in the opening epigraph was harder to achieve because there were fewer opportunities for the school community to gather collectively in a setting designed to value everyone's thoughts and ideas.

While many other schools use an advisory curriculum (although it is implemented differently across school sites), Prep is one of the few public schools in New York City that actually includes Town Meetings/Quads in the weekly schedule. The James Baldwin School, which spun out of Humanities Prep, does this as well. Students' reactions show that Town Meetings/Quads at Prep are an integral space to cultivate voice and participate in decisionmaking; Prep students saw Town Meetings/Quads as a crucial space where they felt validated, their opinions mattered, and they were intellectually challenged.

THE FAIRNESS COMMITTEE: RESTORATIVE APPROACHES

> Please keep doing Fairness. I'm telling you, it works, even though I hated it at the time. When I was having some issues in Mark's class, he took me to Fairness . . . it showed me that you cared, but even more, it brought me closer to my teachers. I felt closer to Mark and Harry after that. (Diego, alumnus, interview, January 11, 2008)

The plea above was made by Diego during a meeting with staff at an annual Prep Alumni Day, when former students come back to engage with their old classmates, offer advice, and meet with teachers. Also simply known as "Fairness," the Fairness Committee is seen by students and staff as a crucial reflective democratic practice at Prep, in that it helps cultivate voice, allows for questioning, and reinforces a caring community. Often framed as a form of "restorative justice," Fairness is a mechanism through which students can discuss with one another, and with teachers, violations of the community's Core Values and brainstorm alternatives and solutions to these dilemmas.[2] Examples where a student or teacher might be taken to Fairness include inappropriate language, missing class, and vandalism. When a committee is convened, students and teachers are encouraged to ask questions, listen to all parties, and help uncover what transpired. The structure strives to emphasize process and real dialogue over product and fixed outcome, so the end result is sui generis to each particular Committee meeting (Hantzopoulos, 2006).

Teachers and administrators around the country are increasingly interested in learning more about the practice, particularly as they are becoming ever more frustrated with punitive policies that seem only to marginalize and disengage youth from school culture (see Hantzopoulos, 2013). At Prep, however, Fairness goes beyond discipline; it is a mechanism to build community, cultivate student voice, and raise critical consciousness. Because the Fairness Committee brings in the voices of students who often are marginalized by traditional disciplinary practices, the intention is to validate students as thinkers and decisionmakers, reinforcing the idea that they have a stake and voice in their communities. As Harry, Prep's founder, indicated, the Fairness Committee is another way to extend humanizing relationships and assimilate some of the Core Values of the school:

> Alternative ways of (re)socializing kids are one way of bringing kids into closer contact with community values, what's typically known as discipline. I think Fairness is a great example of that. But on another level altogether is something that Kathy once said is humane conversations, and we really started out that way. Before there was Fairness . . . before there were a lot of things, there were constant humane conversations with kids . . . they do buy in to some extent, you know. They take Fairness seriously and they talk about some of the values, or they tell us, you know, "where's the Core Values?" (interview, June 15, 2007)

Thus fairness at Prep goes beyond "discipline" and community norm violations and as implied by Harry, it is another way to nurture the types of bonds Diego described, to build community with students, and their thoughts and reflections, at the center. While a student or teacher may take another student or teacher to Fairness if there is a perceived violation of a Core Value, the processes and outcomes of the "committee hearings" often deepen the level of engagement between the two parties. As Lawrence, the former principal, said:

> Well, over the years, we've always worked hard to make "student input" happen more consistently. Of course Fairness is huge . . . both in terms of the medium and the message. We take it so seriously and [it] also goes beyond the idea that there's just engagement in classes. There are those expectations of involvement . . . I guess [it is] because the expectations are so strong that . . . the "normal" processes in schools are enhanced because of that. (interview, March 19, 2007)

Lawrence suggests that the Fairness Committee more or less supports the other processes, values, and structures that exist in the school.

In one Fairness session I observed, Paul took his best friend to Fairness for violating the Core Value "respect for the intellect." The friend, Joe, had begun to frequently miss school; he was slipping academically and becoming emotionally withdrawn. Paul was concerned that his friend was going to drop out and wanted to have a larger intervention, so he brought him to Fairness. In that meeting, the students and teachers who were present tried to get to the heart of Joe's problems so appropriate steps could be taken to reintegrate him back into school. In the end, the Fairness Committee formed an academic advisory plan for Joe; it involved interventions and checks from

Joe's advisor and also from Paul. While Fairness was often difficult for students, many echoed Diego's claim in the opening quote of this section that "it works, even though I hated it at the time" (interview, January 11, 2008).

Students describe Fairness as a safe place that allows them to reflect and raise awareness regarding behaviors that might harm others, or even bring harm to themselves. For instance, Alejo described being taken to Fairness not only as a way to be called out on something, but also as a way to validate his own humanity:

> I remember that because every time that I would violate [a Core Value], I would be called on it in Fairness . . . I think they were good things to have. . . . And then here with those Core Values, it is more like you're a person. You're your own person, as opposed to being anything specific. (interview, April 24, 2007)

Because Fairness seeks to unearth the truth(s) of a situation, the process encompasses multiple community perspectives, thereby attempting to dismantle hierarchical impositions of truth. Thus, Alejo describes his humanity being validated because he was included in the process, even when he was "accused" of violating a Core Value. Similarly, Jenkins attributed his personal growth to Fairness:

> When I first came here I was . . . a time bomb. But, 'cause we had Town Meeting, 'cause we used to debate about stuff, I was very, like, reluctant to hear anyone else's view and like, "uhhh, everyone shut up." And I went to Fairness like four times, and as I began to be in this environment more, I began to learn that even though there is the factor of freedom of speech, and you are liberated, there are boundaries within liberation that have to be understood. So I think that's what I learned the most from here. (interview, March 25, 2007)

Through dialogical engagement with other members of the community, Jenkins feels that he became more aware of the effects of his actions on others. Others students also appreciate how Fairness allows for the contention of multiple perspectives. For example, Luis relates the following: "I especially loved the whole thing [of] Fairness. Fairness was a pointed concept to me, because . . . usually people just get suspended. But Fairness actually allows people to speak both sides of their story . . . and it's a good process to go through, you know, for people to have their voice heard" (interview, March 13, 2007). Luis's emphasis on voice, the voices of both someone "taken" to Fairness and someone sitting on the panel, exemplifies how democracy is practiced in the space. As Kevin stated, "Prep definitely taught students about fairness, diversity, and democracy" (interview, December 20, 2006). Adrian, a science teacher, holds a similar view of Fairness:

That's a great means for negotiating all this pluralism. There is so much room for interpretation around this stuff in general and if we are in fact trying to teach judgment to kids then Fairness becomes a place for those kinds of mature discussions to take place when there's a difference of opinion about how we ought to behave. I think it's great. It engages people. It demands that people think about their behavior as opposed to just fearing punishment. (interview, May 8, 2007)

Tania, another teacher, noted that the Fairness Committee allows students to grapple with the Core Values so they can be "their higher selves" (interview, June 5, 2007). In one case, Luther, a 10th-grader at the time, took himself to Fairness for breaking a school window. While the ensuing Fairness Committee was used as a means to explore exactly what transpired, it was also a self-selected space for him to come to terms with his actions and provide himself with a more complete picture. During that session, the members of the Committee learned that the day before he broke the window, Luther's family received notice that they were being kicked out of their shelter; they had no place to go. While this did not fully excuse his actions, the Committee was able to discuss more fully and fairly what the consequences should be, as well as more constructive ways to deal with anger.

These examples show that a Fairness Committee potentially can democratize and humanize discipline. Incidents that require discipline still happen at Prep, but the Fairness Committee is an alternative way to deal with those incidents so that students are less likely to become further alienated from the community. Moreover, the Fairness Committee at Prep represents a desegregated, integrated space in which young people's relational skills can be nurtured under the conditions of sense of community, analysis of difference, and investment in democracy (Fine et al., 1997).

CONCLUSION: THE CASE FOR PARTICIPATORY SCHOOLING

Through enacting a participatory curriculum that validates students' humanity and worth, and teaches them to do the same to others, Prep exemplifies the praxis of HRE. While present educational policies narrowly focus on testing and discipline, despite evidence that these initiatives have only exacerbated inequities in schooling, mainstreaming HRE is a sound strategy for public schools seeking to broaden and deepen students' educational access and attainment. In this sense, HRE, buttressed by and enacted through intentional participatory spaces like those described in this section, not only fosters human rights learning, but also serves as a mechanism to include students who have been demoralized by school and teach them to take ownership of their own learning process and decisions as they learn the value of their unique voices.

Various studies (Apple & Beane, 2007; Knoester, 2012) show how democratized spaces and processes are instrumental in building school culture, and work well in those specific environments. Many schools utilize interesting forms of student governance in determining school policy. Prep offers specific and unique direct and participatory practices for schools to consider when they are determining the most appropriate overall curriculum. Although many schools offer Advisory in some form, Prep's approach might inspire schools currently using it as homeroom to reconsider that space as one that can center student voice and participation. Schools often are challenged by spatial and scheduling logistics, but there also might be ways to consciously create gatherings like Quads/Town Meetings to prioritize student participation in school life.

Perhaps the most salient example of how participatory spaces can spread is Prep's Fairness Committee. When I first wrote about the Fairness Committee in 2006 for *Rethinking Schools*, Prep was the only public high school in New York City that used such a structured process for restorative discipline and justice. At that time, zero-tolerance policies and police presence in NYC public schools were on the rise, and progressive educators and students were actively seeking alternatives to counter these trends. Groups like the New York Collective of Radical Educators, Teachers Unite, and NESRI organized workshops, roundtables, and discussions on restorative practices in schools. According to Anna Bean of Teachers Unite (personal communication, May 2015), an informal poll garnered from trainings they have done shows that more than 75 public middle and high schools in the city have incorporated some sort of restorative disciplinary practices, and roughly 25 schools have integrated restorative practices more fully and comprehensively. While not all of those schools use a full HRE approach in other areas, these numbers show that HRE practices can be implemented in small ways to transform schools into more humanizing and dignified spaces. Through these examples, and through the advocacy of groups like Dignity in Schools and Teachers Unite, the New York City Council announced in June 2015 that will it begin funding restorative justice pilot programs in 15 schools.

All of the participatory structures mentioned in this chapter are worthy of replication. While how such structures are implemented will be contingent upon the context, this chapter shows that strategic participatory spaces are powerful tools to foster critical thinking and engagement among students. In the following chapter, I look more closely at how students viewed the overall participatory culture at Prep and critically examine some of the tensions that arise when this type of engagement is enacted in a school setting.

CHAPTER 8

Navigating Multiple and Complex Social Environments

HRE, Social Change, and Broader Civic Engagement

In the summer of 2013, Abigail, a former Prep student now in her late 20s, contacted me. She was applying for a job at a prominent human rights organization and sought advice about the process. We had been in and out of touch over the years, and I remembered that she had expressed interest in human rights work when I initially interviewed her via email in 2007. At the time, Abigail was living in Nicaragua and Costa Rica, collecting oral histories of migrant families and working with "NGOs and private foundations to see what people are doing to combat some of the pressing human rights issues here on a grassroots or local level" (personal communication, March 27, 2007). Like many of the students described in the previous chapter, Abigail credited Prep for influencing her to be "a more socially and politically conscious person" and "an active participant in the global community," catalyzing her interest in effecting change.

This chapter considers the role of human rights education in students' lives beyond school, and offers insight and recommendations related to how schools and educators can use holistic HRE approaches to help students develop skills of communication, critical thinking, self-awareness, and activism that help them navigate complex social environments. Students leaving HRE-centered schools tend to express desires to effect positive change in society, work toward dismantling unjust structures, or simply give back to their communities in some tangible way—but they also brush up against realities that challenge their assumptions that multiple voices are welcome and that change is possible. This friction is particularly pronounced when young people contend with power dynamics and larger structural inequities, within and beyond school, that inhibit their sense of agency. Nonetheless, I argue that while students sometimes feel restricted by what they are able to do in these situations, their schooling has given them relevant experiential knowledge that they both display and convey as they negotiate these tensions, often to their advantage.

Schools that use a holistic HRE framework are manifestations of sites in which—and by which—agency is negotiated, contested, and remade, often in unexpected, unassuming, and contradictory ways, and there is much to be learned from this process. In this vein, I assert that the tools, practices, and values of HRE help students develop the skills needed to adapt to the different contexts they must continually navigate. I also make the case that educators must continually and reflectively pay attention to the varied meanings that students ascribe to their own experiences with this type of schooling, in order to shed light on their students' particular educational needs. Thus, I close the chapter by highlighting HRE strategies that schools can employ to help students reconcile the complex social realms they navigate and negotiate social transitions more effectively.

CRITICAL CONSCIOUSNESS AND BROADER SOCIAL CHANGE: A COLLECTIVE ENDEAVOR

The way students learn from and in their classes, and in the nonacademic spaces discussed in earlier chapters, crystallize into an overall experience at Prep whereby and wherein students collectively find their voices and better understand the complex world in which they live. Repeatedly, when asked what they learned that stuck with them, students gave responses like that of Reneka, who quipped, "To speak my mind, I guess" (interview, March 12, 2007). Deena, who was still attending Prep at the time, said, "It helped me become a better person and to find my voice and know that I have the right to share that. It has had an amazing impact on my life and [Prep] has been by far the best school choice" (interview, December 20, 2006). Austin, a recent alumnus, explained in a survey (2007) that the overall school culture enabled students to gain comfort speaking up: "In a way, I believed that I learned to be a bit more vocal. The overall discussion-based format certainly made me more comfortable voicing my opinions." Other participants explained that their schooling at Prep gave them the confidence and skills to speak up in broader arenas beyond the school, as well. For instance, Taina, an alumna, reported:

> The school made me feel a real sense of community unlike the other high school I attended in Miami.[1] It helped me with public speaking, which was very beneficial to me when I entered college. I never realized how important Prep was until I left, unfortunately. The student–teacher relationship or friendship rather was extremely impactful to my life and is very much valued. (survey, 2007)

Specifically talking about the value of the public speaking skills she gained at Prep, Taina ties those skills to the school's overall culture when she mentions the "sense of community" and "relationships" that she developed at Prep.

Several other students also described Prep as a place that strengthened their "communication skills." For instance, Stacy, a senior, specifically mentioned that all of the structures, formal and informal, reinforced one another to help her become "more social" and communicative:

> I think that just helps everyone just grow on their speaking skills, being social, 'cause people would join the conversation and you know, you gain new relationships working with people like that. And I've just learned a lot, like meeting these teachers. You know, I'm able to communicate with adults like that I have never been able to with any other kind of person before I came to this school. So, I've definitely like been able to speak to the teachers whenever I feel like it. If I'm going through a problem, I can just talk to the teachers and Advisory if I don't have a class, during break, lunch, anything, so I've really grown like in all different aspects. (focus group, May 2, 2007)

Stacy equates being able to communicate with "growth." Other students, such as Sebastien, noted the same phenomenon:

> It's basically the same thing with me. Like, I've grown academically and just as a person being in Humanities Prep because, like Stacy, I've always been a person that would talk, but I speak up at times, but like this school has given me like the courage to just speak up whenever I feel it's needed and not like hold my breath for anybody. And especially like when I feel something needs to be said, I'll do it now because I've learned to go into the Quads, classes, and even after school, like we'll have in-depth conversations with students and teachers . . . and the topic will come up from any student in the school and we will just sit there for hours just going at it. (focus group, May 2, 2007)

Sebastien references how various forms of school life and school culture intersect to help him feel more confident about expressing his ideas. Jessie, a senior, couched growth in similar discourse that links education, personal relationships, and public speaking as catalysts for academic and interpersonal growth:

> I would say yeah . . . I think Prep allows a lot of individuals to grow . . . just differently with education and personal relationships and, as she [another focus group participant] said, public speaking and just elaborating on your thoughts and views. But I just think that I love Prep for what it is. (focus group, May 2, 2007)

Many students and alumni went further to mention that the participatory culture and the types of interactions encouraged at Prep not only allowed them to express their opinions, but also allowed them to learn *how* to express their opinions in ways that were constructive and helped them achieve their goals. Terri, an alumna who became a kindergarten teacher and union activist, expressed this view very clearly:

> After 4 years of college and my pursuit of a career in education I must say Prep was my best educational experience. It made me a better writer, communicator, and introduced me to my first adult relationships—ones I truly value. Prep prepared me for college. Prep taught me to question. Prep taught me to think. Prep has had a significant impact on the person that I am today. (survey, 2007)

Marianna, another alumna, stated:

> To take the respect part of the conversations that they teach you—in Advisory and just in general in Prep Central—and the openness that you have with your teachers at Prep seriously, because there are the clues and cues and social hints that they are giving you at this time that will enable you to interact with others in a professional, adult, respectful, courteous manner that you need in other parts of your life. (interview, March 29, 2007)

Amelia, also an alumna, was more specific about the nature of the "clues and cues and social hints" that Marianna referenced in her statement:

> It is kind of hard to gauge the impact that Prep had on me because I was home schooled before attending high school. Coming to Prep was really my first time interacting with people outside of my family, so a lot of the things I learned at Prep were things about interacting with other people. For example, I learned that people like it if you speak to their faces when you are commenting on something they said, while you are still in their presence (instead of looking over their heads), something like this seems like common sense, but it's something that I really didn't quite understand. Learning to speak to people has had a tremendous impact on my life, specifically in that since I have left, I have gotten all positions, academic and otherwise, that I've interviewed for. I was also really shy when I came to Prep, and now I am not any more. So, Prep had a strong positive impact on me about things of this nature. (interview, March 11, 2007)

While Amelia insinuates that home schooling previously isolated her and prevented her from "interacting with people," other students who *had* been through the institution of schooling actually described their experiences very similarly. For instance, Sammy, an alumnus who transferred from a prestigious public high school, said:

> Prep also did wonders for my social life and pushed me out of my shyness, which people often mistook for aloofness, and showed me that people are people and can be talked to and bonded with no matter what their outer demeanor and appearance may be. (interview, April 28, 2007)

Many students specifically recount Prep as a schooling experience that made them view and reflect on "the world" differently. In Chapter 6 students and alumni described developing critical thinking skills as a result of what transpired in their classes and the academic curriculum itself; many also suggested that Prep's broader culture of participation and intellectual discourse encourage students to continually question what is presented as truth. The alumni in the following three excerpts, for example, ultimately attributed their more nuanced worldview to the participatory culture of the school:

> Also, I learned about issues in the world that I wasn't even aware of until I came here because at my other school we didn't really talk about that. It was all just from-the-book stuff. (Lisa, interview, March 27, 2007)

> This school made me want to learn about what is going on around the world beyond NYC. [It] opened my eyes to issues going on around the world. (Lexus, survey, 2007)

> I think this school educated me on topics I would not have cared . . . about, so they made me more informed of the world and the issues taking place. (Dionne, survey, 2007)

In many ways, these experiences parallel critical pedagogy notions of "liberation," although in this case the "awareness" not only is contingent on the student–teacher relationship, but also includes a larger community of learners for whom dialogue and curiosity are part of the overall school culture. For many students and alumni, "awareness" led to deeper analysis and questioning of taken-for-granted truths, what Wright (2015) coins sociopolitical analysis skills. Kevin, an alumnus, described the school as a community that helped him to "not accept something at face value" (interview, December 20, 2006). Luis described:

> I mean, it's a high school, so you obviously wanna educate people, but I think, you know, as far as, you know, asking questions and asking why,

you know, like learning that . . . we learned here that education doesn't stop at school. You know, in education you can learn things outside. You can learn things from anywhere . . . just asking questions and you know, paying attention to the answers. (interview, March 13, 2007)

Beyond normalizing a process of analysis that encourages everyone to interrogate taken-for-granted assumptions about "the world," several students and alumni mentioned that Prep also challenges students to question their own particular histories and narratives. One alumna, Rebecca, gave the example of how being at Prep gave her a framework to view Jamaica, her ancestral country, differently:

My critique of capitalism definitely came from Prep. Nobody believes me but I think this school is secretly communist [laugh]. . . . When I went to Jamaica last fall, I had fun, but saw my country in a different way. I noticed disparities between the rich and the poor. I was there for 11 days and saw *so* much. (interview, January 5, 2007)

She described being on the top of a hill and noting the spatial juxtaposition of two-room shacks on one side and fancy mansions and resorts on the other. While she admitted that tourism generates money for the country, she also described the tourism industry as potentially "exploiting the country": "People who live across the street from Margaritaville [a popular club for tourists] have never been to the beach because they have to pay. As a kid, I just did not have that view of Jamaica" (interview, January 5, 2007). Rebecca expressed gratitude that her experience at the school not only led her to think about the world differently, but specifically led her to think about *her* world differently.

Some students and alumni felt that, beyond getting them to think more critically, Prep's culture of participation facilitates empathy among the student body and catalyzes many students to become activists. Rebecca explained that Prep helped her gain empathy:

I came into Prep, I was always opinionated. But I wasn't always open to other people's ideas. A lot of the things that I thought were wrong or bad and I just didn't like and that was it, and if you didn't like it then okay. But now I'm open to other people's ideas and to being okay [with] different people having different perspectives on things. (interview, January 5, 2007)

Similarly, Deena, who describes herself as coming from a tolerant background, suggested that being at Prep taught her to be more open to people who did not share her ideas and perspectives. Deena explained that in middle school she had been intolerant of those who were "closed-minded," whereas at Prep, the sites dedicated to contestation and discourse challenged her:

> Prep gave me the opportunity, through places like Town Meeting, and Quad, and Advisory, to be a little bit more understanding towards views that were a little bit different from my own. . . . It taught me to be able to view things from someone else's perspective, to not get so frustrated because it is important to not get so frustrated and to understand where they are coming from. It also taught me that there is more than one truth in the world. And it taught me to be more . . . open-minded [laughing] even though I am from the most open-minded family. (interview, December 20, 2006)

This is particularly noteworthy because Deena later explained that the Core Values of Prep were similar to the values of her family. Yet, because she was part of a more ideologically diverse community at Prep than at home, she was forced to contend with a greater variety of perspectives and life experiences—and that process was beneficial.

Luis was one of several alumni who described how his experiences at Prep contributed to his desire to effect change:

> Prep changed my life. It made me see the world in a different light. It allowed me to ask what I can do for others rather than what they can do for me. . . . I mean, I think I've matured . . . I started to see that, you know, I can influence the world just as much as people influence me. . . . I didn't think that when I first came here. I thought, I'm just an ant in a colony . . . playing a role . . . but I know that, you know, I can actually do stuff now to influence other people and to make life better for others. (interview, March 13, 2007)

Luis, in fact, said that his schooling at Prep compelled him to want to go into teaching as an act of social change; he ended up studying education at Hunter College. Other responses from alumni and students illuminated similar hopes about transforming society. Queenia, an alumna, shared:

> I think [Prep] changed my perspective on life and what my potential as a human being is in this world. . . . Like, I loved when we were protesting the Regents exams and me and a couple other students actually wrote letters and we went and we read the letters at City Hall. . . . We actually went and we read those letters as part of our campaign . . . you hear about people doing these amazing things, these protests and these campaigns and just taking up these causes that they feel strongly for, and you never realize that those people are the same people as you. There's nothing about them that's extraordinary, *except that they choose to be*

extraordinary people [emphasis added]. I think that should be Prep's motto 'cause I feel like everyone I've gone to school with has come out of Prep such an interesting and evolved person . . . and then seeing myself as an adult after Prep and just hearing me talk and hearing so much of Prep in what I've learned. That's my favorite part of being [part] of a school like that. (interview, May 6, 2007)

By engaging students in ways that push them to develop and try different strategies to achieve social change, Prep helps each student realize her/his own ability to be influential in arenas few of them had even imagined.

NEGOTIATING PARTICIPATORY ENGAGEMENT
AT SCHOOL WHEN TENSIONS ARISE

During the first weeks of my fieldwork at Prep, the school was subject to a new NYC Department of Education policy; police officers with portable metal detectors began conducting unannounced sweeps of students and their bags at middle schools and high schools throughout the city (Herszenhorn, 2006). When the police and the roving metal detectors showed up on the seventh day of school, several students from Prep and another similarly themed school in the building began to organize and protest. Some refused to go through the metal detectors and were detained. Others paraded up and down the street, holding signs that stated they were being criminalized. One student contacted her mother to pressure the media to come bear witness at the school. The police, who were not used to this response at schools, phoned the Head of Security at the Department of Education. More executives showed up from the central office, and soon phone calls were made to the principals at these two schools, both of whom were still settling into their jobs (one was in his first year and the other in his second). They were told to expect severe repercussions, maybe even job loss, if student protests did not stop. As a result, students were persuaded by staff to stop and comply. Some acquiesced to these demands, while others remained confused and angry. Many asked questions like, "Isn't this what we are supposed to be doing if we feel that injustice is happening? Isn't this what we learned here?"

This illustrative situation brings to the forefront complex tensions between "reality" and "hope for change." While Prep tried to mediate this tension by holding an emergency Town Meeting in which students were able to voice their frustration and anger, students were still asked not to protest on or around the school grounds. Students were encouraged to meet over the course of the week to develop other strategies, but one student was dissatisfied and accused the school administration of being complicit in bringing the metal detectors to the school. This student's accusation sheds light on how students' desires and administrative mandates are often fraught with tension in quotidian interactions. When clashes like this occurred, Prep students often were able to negotiate these tensions to their advantage, even when they felt that their desires were inconsistent with those of their teachers. For example, during auditions for Prep's annual talent show, a few students wanted to stage a wrestling match in the dramatic style of the World Wide Wrestling Federation. While some teachers felt that this inherently would contradict Prep's Core Values (in particular, a commitment to peace), the students presented a case for how they would integrate the Core Values into their presentation without any actual fighting, just fake acrobatics and some movement. This posed a dilemma for the teachers: If the school is democratic and the students were attempting to (re)define the Core Values in their presentation, could/should the teachers prevent it from happening? Even students not involved in the project were weighing in on the debate, insisting that it would be hypocritical not to allow them their chance on stage.

In the end, the staff decided to let them do it, under supervision, although one staff member adamantly disagreed. Taking seriously the staff concerns, the two student "wrestlers" actually wove into their act a skit about "Old Prep" vs. "New Prep," a common discussion that year about how new students were not as acculturated to the school as "old" students. Despite a few jarring thumps and flips, the students created a performance that ultimately emphasized unity between new and old students. Thus, they endeavored to use this "wrestling match" as a way to highlight an underlying issue in the school that often was discussed in sanctioned formats such as Town Meeting, and concurrently put on a spectacular wrestling show.

Another example of community contention surfaced when a prominent guest author came to the school, although this discord was left less resolved. After weeks of preparation and reading his book, students in four Advisories had prepared a forum to host the author. This included a "book talk" with a catered-by-students reception after the author's presentation, during which they intended to discuss his book and share their projects with him. When the author arrived at the book talk, he told students that he did not have to talk about the book and could just as well talk about boxing, and he peppered his speech with harsh curse words and anecdotes about being young and mischievous. Some students thought this was hilarious, whereas others were offended at what they perceived to be his lack of respect for them. One teacher in the forum challenged the author openly, letting him know that his lack of preparation or willingness to even talk about being a writer insulted the students' intelligence. The author seemed humored by this challenge and presented himself as someone who was in solidarity with the students, whom he assumed were more interested in hearing about boxing. He continued to proceed with what he wanted to talk about, despite the fact that many students did want to talk about his book.

After the "book talk," students went back to their Advisories. The topic of the author's visit dominated each Advisory discussion. More important, other debates also emerged, such as the appropriateness of cursing (when, why, and where) and whether the author was "keeping it real" or acting condescending toward the students. Students went back and forth on these issues for the entire week, some changing positions, others adamantly defending the author's right to free speech. What was perhaps most revelatory about this process was that it was organic, there was a space for everyone to process it, and there was no fixed outcome of these conversations. Many people believed, for different reasons, different things. Thus, this was a clear example of how a school community can use unresolved tension and disagreement—between students and faculty but also among students themselves—to help students explore different ways of thinking about topics that emerge from a contentious situation. While most teachers felt strongly about their positions, there was no expectation that they or the students would, or should, arrive at a singular truth, but rather that everyone should grapple together with the realities of the situation at hand.

When the stakes were higher for students and teachers, though, unresolved tension sometimes caused deep frustration. For instance, there were times when negotiation over the shared space of Prep Central created conflict among students and teachers. During school hours, students were required to have a free period or a note from their teacher to be in there working. After school hours, students had 40 minutes for relaxation time, after which, as the sign looming on the wall indicated, Prep Central was for "quiet and meaningful conversation or work." Although students and staff alike tended to view Prep Central as a positive space, these competing uses sometimes led to power struggles between students and teachers over the use of space. One afternoon, students were upset that they had to leave the space so teachers could finish their work:

> Later on that afternoon, at 4:30, I engaged in a discussion with students about staying late in Prep Central. This transpired because they were about to play cards, were screaming loudly, and asked to leave. . . . They brought up several issues and emotions, like "We feel unwanted" (Demetri), "We have no place to go" (Matt), "Why can't we go in the music room?" (Randa), "These are moments that we want to cherish" (Matt). In fact, one student even said, "If we were talking about politics or something else, the teachers would let us stay." (fieldnotes, March 22, 2007)

The tension that manifested in this instance shows some of the difficulties of negotiating a communal space, even though it is a cornerstone of how democracy is perceived and enacted in the school. As critiques of critical pedagogy illuminate, the perception of egalitarian student–teacher relationships erodes when needs and desired outcomes conflict (see Ellsworth, 1989; Gore, 1992). Nonetheless, students and teachers tried to find common solutions when there was an issue over the use of Prep Central, so negotiations over the space did not always break down. Another example from my fieldnotes illustrates how one such negotiation was resolved after students asked to go into another empty room to hang out, as long as one available teacher could be present.

Collectively, these examples show the myriad types of outcomes that manifest when there are clashes over ideals. While they illuminate some inherent power dynamics that exist, despite attempts to "equalize them," among students and teachers, these examples also reveal that the school space itself was also a site of contestation. While no current or former students interviewed talked about these or other struggles over ideals, my fieldnotes indicate that they are common experiences in the school.

ALUMNI EXPERIENCES NAVIGATING SOCIAL REALMS BEYOND SCHOOL

What many alumni did express was the realization that there were larger constraints on their ideals or their sense of agency after they left Prep. Many alumni described feeling charged with optimism when they left the school, but becoming tainted with cynicism when they encountered obstacles that challenged their commitment or ability to effect change. For instance, Antoinette, a student who transferred to Prep as a junior from a specialized high school in NYC, was studying abroad in Jerusalem. When asked to describe Prep in her survey, she wrote:

> Prep reinvigorated a love of learning for me. The teachers encouraged me to look at the world around me, ask questions, and initiate positive change. One of the most important lessons that I learned was that activism did not have to be only big issues that you hear about on TV or marching with signs, but could be as small as helping someone in the neighborhood, or making the school look nicer. By making activism possible, Prep instilled in me the need to always be working towards positive change. Living now in Jerusalem I struggle with this, as it is hard for me to walk to Arab [Palestinian] neighborhoods and see poverty and discrimination, but be unable to help without putting myself in danger. I am sure, though, if I look, I will find ways to work in small ways. (2007)

Antoinette describes the difficulty of being an agent of change when larger societal forces prevent her from even engaging in the world in ways she has come to find familiar.

Since this excerpt is not from an interview but rather from a survey, I was unable to explore why she felt there was "danger"; nonetheless, she conveys feeling that there are real obstacles to her sense of agency in specific contexts.

Rebecca, another alumna, also expressed that she sometimes felt she lacked power to initiate change in her post-Prep environment:

> Humanities Preparatory Academy impacted me by allowing me to become aware of the social issues that mattered in this society. The school sheltered me, however, from other institutions where my voice may not have been heard and caused me to be aware of the issues in our society that need to be changed. (survey, 2007)

Like Antoinette, Rebecca describes feeling inhibited by external structures and institutions that limit her "voice." Her comment about being "sheltered" reveals an interesting paradox. When I asked her to explain further, she described her rural college as a "rich White school" in which she, as an urban Black woman, struggles to find a place where her voice is not institutionally silenced. It is noteworthy, though, that Rebecca's survey response intimates that this very tension allows her to understand what else "need[s] to be changed," suggesting that she has not lost hope for herself as an agent of change.

It was common for alumni to speak specifically about how they were disappointed with the cultures of new institutions that often did not reflect the same values as Prep. Because Fairness is viewed very positively as a forum within Prep, some alumni think it should be utilized in spaces beyond the school. For example, one alumna, Amelia, was particularly frustrated with the way the administration at her college dealt with issues of race and gender:

> I've been like yelling at . . . people about what's wrong with the diversity at the school. I mentioned the Prep situation. . . . You know how Prep has the whole Fairness thing? Well, School X doesn't have anything like that . . . for example, there was a guy who had a crush on me in the beginning of last term, and I didn't say hi to him one day and he came with a really powerful water gun and squirted me . . . and I was really angry . . . and there's nothing you can do for anything that's not, like, where you have like a physical scar. . . . It just seems like there's no accountability for anything that goes on. And even last term a sophomore actually got on the radio here . . . and he, a White person, [said something racist]! And there were no consequences, it just makes me angry, nobody did anything. I really feel like at Prep, if you would do something to disrespect the community there's going to be consequences, even if you don't get in trouble by the teachers at Prep so much, the community thinks you're a jerk. But instead, here, you're just walking around, partying it up, having fun; it just makes me so mad. (interview, March 11, 2007)

Some current students, on the other hand, believe that Fairness is not going to be an option beyond the walls of Prep. As Victor, a senior, put it: "I mean, no, there's no Fairness anywhere outside. If there's a problem and you don't resolve it, then you gotta fight. That's it. There's no Fairness" (interview, May 22, 2007). This statement reveals both his faith in the Fairness Committee at school and his cynicism about applying this approach elsewhere.

Other alumni noted the intergenerational and diverse community at Prep as being uncommon and described how difficult it has been to integrate themselves into other, homogenous environments. For example, Dalia described how she felt shocked at the beginning of college when she could not connect with other students:

> I was kind of thrown into the real world . . . it was a commuter school so it was really hard to meet people. So my first freshman year in college I absolutely detested the school [her college] . . . it was very bizarre for me 'cause I just went from a school that had so much warmth, and liveliness, to a school that didn't. It almost felt like being at [her previous mainstream public school] again, not at Humanities Prep, but a very rigid, segregated environment, and I was like, "Isn't Prep prepping me for college? It's not!" (interview, February 15, 2007)

Dalia later explained that she had negotiated this tension by becoming involved in Arab American clubs and networks in her school and in the community. In fact, at the time of my research, she was directing a documentary about the fetish-ization of Arab American culture in mainstream American culture. She concluded, "You know, it [Prep] did actually [prepare me for college]; the way we interacted with one another, whether it was with students or teachers . . . being in college long enough and being a part of organizations, and functions, and classes, you start to see how that really preps you for college." Dalia was, at the end, very articulate about connecting her experience with HRE approaches at Prep to her decision to take an active approach to navigating a less welcoming community.

Much like Dalia, Rebecca, the alumna who mentioned in a previous quote that she sometimes felt she lacked power to initiate change in her post-Prep environment, ultimately adapted by looking for a community that might embrace her voice. Unable to find quite the right match in her immediate environment, Rebecca joined an African American community service–oriented sorority at another college in the vicinity. By turning to affinity groups reflective of an aspect of their personal identities, these young women actively sought to build community in contexts where they felt better positioned to initiate change within institutions and communities they perhaps perceived as racist or sexist. Their actions and words suggest that rather than losing hope for change when they were confronted with new

environments that did not seem to welcome their voices, these young people found new and creative ways to mediate these tensions. Moreover, it is
important to point out that students clearly do not live in a vacuum while
attending Prep. There are other societal factors that students had to contend
with on a daily basis while attending the school, many of which are in conflict with the type of community values that exist there. Nonetheless, their
description of life post-Prep accentuates that students may have had higher
expectations of their new environments because of their experiences at Prep.

STRATEGIES THAT HELP STUDENTS BETTER NAVIGATE TRANSITIONS AND SOCIAL ENVIRONMENTS BEYOND SCHOOL

Many of the societal factors students had to contend with on a daily basis
were/are in direct and obvious conflict with Prep's community values. Students and alumni described times when their perceptions of fairness and justice differed from the perceptions of their teachers, as well as circumstances
and structural norms beyond Prep that were/are beyond their control. Thus,
despite Prep's attempts to create a humanizing and democratizing environment, alumni and students still brush up against values antithetical to those
that the school promotes. This reality led a few students and alumni to describe Prep as an idealistic place removed from real-world contexts rife with
structural inequities that inhibit their sense of agency.

Importantly, though, while students and alumni often feel restricted by
what they are able (or not able) to do when they encounter such obstacles,
many of them also report being able to negotiate these tensions to their
advantage by finding ways to mediate their own mismatched expectations.
While this raises broader questions about the extent to which education can
be transformative in light of larger structural inequalities, these students'
stories also illuminate some of the HRE skills that potentially help them cir-
cumvent perceived and actual barriers and navigate obstacles without losing
hope. By centering the localized understandings reflected in participant experiences, the data show that although enacting HRE education in schools
is not entirely liberating for participants, the HRE goals can be achieved in
public schools even though the enactment of democratic and human rights
education is often messy and never complete.

Given this, there are some concrete measures that might assuage the
tensions that inevitably arise when democratized processes are intentionally
enacted in a school space, and also better prepare students to navigate transitions and social environments beyond school. First, former and current
students at Prep repeatedly spoke of the importance of school culture and
intergenerational democratic spaces for questioning and contestation. Several were concerned that Town Meetings, which they perceived to be vital
for democratic participation and academic engagement, were becoming less

frequent. Because of the resoundingly positive attitudes about these structures, Prep must ensure that they continue, even as the students and staff change throughout the years—and other schools can use this model to create their own participatory spaces and structures. A formal New Teacher Orientation at the beginning of each academic year could be co-led and designed by students and seasoned staff so that all members of the community are reminded of and more easily acclimated to the overall school culture. This type of training is vital in any school with a mission that reflects HRE principles in theory and practice.

Schools can employ other strategies to help students reconcile the complex social realms they navigate and negotiate social transitions more effectively. For many years at Prep, numerous students participated in the Community Action Program each semester. Students were placed in off-site, community-based internships with local social justice–oriented nonprofit organizations, while simultaneously participating in community action projects at the school. While the program continues to happen on an ad hoc basis, operationalizing it might provide students with more "reality" and experience with civic engagement beyond the scope of the school, give them structured opportunities to adapt as their sense of agency is challenged and negotiated, and provide them with more insight into social activism in the local community. Although it is not focused on activism per se, Tyner-Mullings (2014) has shown that Central Park East Secondary School's internship program is a pivotal part of the student experience. Schools like Harvest Collegiate and Lyons Community School have truly integrated similar programming into their schedules by having blocks where students are in the field doing community work. Other schools, like City-As-School, actually integrate the internship experience at the center of the academic curriculum (although this is central to the mission of this school). By infusing civic engagement programming into the formal curriculum, schools can provide more opportunities for students to learn experientially and practice activist and professional skills proactively.

Instituting programs like Alumni Day or other times for alumni to speak with current students about their experiences after leaving high school can be instructive and insightful for staff and students alike. At Prep, this came to be instituted as an eagerly anticipated annual event that helps students think through their postsecondary choices and gives staff more information to guide the evolution of school policy. Implementing College Days is a complementary strategy to expose current students to students from various postsecondary institutions to help the former determine their best postsecondary fit. At Prep, while sophomores and juniors were taking the PSAT, freshmen and seniors went on trips to nearby colleges.

In summary, despite some of the challenges, avenues for participatory and civic engagement, even if contradictory and paradoxical at times, are a necessary and fundamental element in a more holistic approach to HRE in schools. In fact, the United Nations Global Education First Initiative (United Nations, 2012) explicitly highlights the importance and urgency of fostering global citizenship through processes that support youth empowerment, agency, and participatory decisionmaking. Prep and the other schools mentioned in this chapter illustrate how this might take shape in practice. In the following chapter, I revisit themes that have emerged throughout the book to reiterate how building a culture of care, respect, critical questioning, and participation collectively contributes to centering the dignity (and ultimately humanity) of students and teachers in these spaces.

CHAPTER 9

Why We Need School Cultures That Center Dignity

What Matters in School Reform

This book weaves stories of possibilities, shedding light on what could occur in urban public schools by sharing narratives of what actually does occur. Too often, dominant narratives about these environments pathologize students and teachers, creating a single story (Adichie, 2013) of public schools, and in particular urban schools, that fails to acknowledge the systemic issues that not only affect teaching and learning, but structure inequity in society at large. This single story often ignores how top-down neoliberal reforms tend to exacerbate inequities and instead frames teachers and students as failures—dismissing, neglecting, and obscuring the beautiful, messy, and vibrant intellectual life that does emerge in these spaces, in spite of efforts to squelch, extinguish, and erase these truths.

Throughout these chapters, I make the humble, simple, and obvious argument that schools and public school reform efforts must center the dignity of students and teachers. I also show the successes and struggles that emerge when schools endeavor to do so. Humanities Preparatory Academy and the other schools mentioned in this book value the academic and emotional well-being of teachers and students by emphasizing practices that help build cultures of care, respect, critical questioning, and participation, undergirded by and aligned with a human rights educational framework. Through enacting a curriculum that centers students' dignity, validates students' humanity and worth, and teaches these students to similarly value others, these schools exemplify the praxis of human rights education. This approach not only disseminates skills and attitudes that build a thriving, diverse intergenerational community that honors the humanity, dignity, and worth of the people within it, but also inherently engages students socially and academically. Prep models the possibilities of urban public schools in terms of its graduation rates and college acceptance rates, using a unique educational model that runs counter to mainstream policies. I therefore consider how the themes that emerged from these alternative narratives might inform a more respectful, holistic, and inclusive educational reform movement in the current climate of neoliberal educational reform. It is my hope that the following generalizable findings will help practitioners from a wide range of contexts reflect on how their schools might benefit from institutionalizing a robust framework and approach grounded in the principles of human rights education.

RELATIONSHIPS MATTER

Throughout my research, a clear pattern emerged: Relationships mark and shape students' schooling experiences in significant ways. Former and current Prep students discussed the fact that positive relationships with teachers and with other students increased their sense of confidence and belonging, and helped them achieve academic success. Teachers at Prep, too, articulated their desire to make students feel comfortable, nurtured, and engaged in the school environment (see Chapter 3). The other schools mentioned in this book have had similarly constructive experiences formally prioritizing relationship building through their missions, practices, structures, and processes.

Much of the literature on caring derives from feminist critiques that challenge conventional approaches to reasoning and morality as ones that are inherently patriarchal and androcentric. By centering caring or relationships, these scholars push for a gendered lens when thinking about moral reasoning or approaches to schooling (see Belenky, Clinchy, Goldberger, & Tarule, 1986; Gilligan, 1982; Noddings, 1992). In recent years, other critical scholars have pushed for deeper intersectional approaches that suggests that *cultural* notions of caring need to be incorporated into scholarship and practice (Antrop-Gonzalez & De Jesús, 2005; De Jesús, 2012; Valenzuela, 1999). As explained in Chapter 4, Bajaj's work (2009) extends the notion of cultural-based caring to context-based caring. After examining how youth in Zambia responded to a peace and justice values–based curriculum, she urges greater consideration of the "larger social, economic, and political structures that surround schools," to allow us to make sense of what happens within them (p. 395). In particular, Bajaj demonstrates how Zambian students, many of whom were orphaned, valued the care they received at this school amid severe economic crisis and the HIV/AIDS pandemic.

While students in NYC do not share that particular context, understanding the context of their lives outside school is incredibly important in thinking about how to build strong relationships and develop a culture of care within schools. While the degree to which particular students may face structural obstacles such as economic and/or social hardship(s) (e.g., incarcerated parents or siblings, homelessness, foster care, responsibility for raising siblings, outside employment, etc.) usually is overlooked in larger educational policy, most of the students who participated in this study did mention feeling neglected, under-recognized, and/or misunderstood at their previous school(s). Finding a school environment where they were nurtured, challenged, and supported was instrumental to their well-being and their academic success, according to their own testimonies. For these reasons, it is absolutely crucial that attention be paid to the social, economic, and cultural experiences of young people when considering how to build meaningful, relevant community practices in a school.

Moreover, students must be valued and acknowledged as more than just students; these young people are multi-faceted human beings that are full of conviction, passion, and complex views about and experiences with the world. Current and former Prep students specifically mentioned that their teachers did value them and gave them "voice" by creating time, space, and energy for less authoritative, nonhierarchical student–teacher relationships. As Freire (1972/2003) posits, such transformed student–teacher relationships did yield more humanizing experiences for these students, influencing their engagement with learning. Many scholars, however, rightfully critique different approaches to how student–teacher relationships are conceptualized and enacted. Bartlett (2005) suggests, for example, that student–teacher relationships that employ a friendship-like strategy often do little to challenge and/or raise critical consciousness among students. Oyler and Becker (1997) echo this sentiment, proposing that teachers often are stuck between the hard place of authoritarian teaching and the soft place of progressive, lenient teaching. Rather than being trapped in this binary, Oyler and Becker theorize a space in which students and teachers share authority (and neither party completely possesses or abdicates it) in order to traverse this tension.

This book has shown how teachers at Prep endeavor, although not without challenge and struggle, to establish and maintain such space in their classrooms and in other places designed to bring members of the school community together. In this sense, creating an *intergenerational, heterogeneous* community in which students and teachers share authority, responsibility, and vulnerability in various arenas of the school is thus a foundational aspect of HRE. The struggle to build just and humane relationships and communities is often messy and complicated; yet, it flourishes when there is willingness to move toward these types of relationships and spaces.

CULTURE MATTERS

Just as relationship-building expectations are fundamental to the establishment of school culture, the intentional HRE-grounded school culture can also engage students and help them learn and grow. Members of the Prep community repeatedly articulated how acceptance, tolerance, and opportunities for personal growth (deeper awareness of and relationship with oneself and with others) contribute to a culture of respect and a sense of community that were fundamental to their academic and social well-being.

The schools featured in the book have clear mission statements, guidelines, and values that ostensibly undergird the structures, processes, and relationships that exist and transpire therein. In fact, the National School Climate Council (2015) published a consensus statement that illuminates the importance of school climate and culture in schools—and suggests guidelines and goals that are already practiced in the schools featured in this book.

Structures such as Town Meetings/Quads and Fairness, as well as other democratized and restorative approaches, solidify a school's value-based culture and facilitate humane and respectful engagement. Without these structures, the same types of student–teacher relationships and intergenerational community may have existed at Prep, but these mechanisms ensured that spaces and time were delineated to formalize them. By ensuring that there were sites for intergencrational democracy and contestation, these structures—and formal spaces such as Advisory and Prep Central—worked as "checks" in the system to ensure the transmission of the desired informal processes. In the case of Prep, both contributed to establishing a vibrant, intellectual school culture that was consistently mentioned by current and former students as being unique and valuable.

I must reiterate that the *intergenerational* and *heterogeneous* aspect of the Prep community was an essential component when students defined the school's positive characteristics. The relationships that transpired and the culture that manifested itself did not emerge just from attempts to create more symmetrical relationships between students and staff, although that was important. Relationship and community building at Prep is the responsibility and function of the entire democratic community. Thus, there is emphasis on creating an inclusive environment in which all actors, in all of their relationships (student–student, student–teacher, teacher–student, and even teacher–teacher), engage in more humane, democratizing, critical discourse. The relationship norms at Prep transcend binary Freirean notions of the ideal student–teacher relationship because they are predicated on Core Values that emphasize interaction within and among all members of the overall community. Rather than emphasizing the role of the teachers, a theory of *collective critical dialogue* shifts responsibility away from any one entity (i.e., the student or the teacher) toward all parties. Town Meetings/Quads, Prep Central, Advisory, and Fairness facilitated this occurrence at the school, and students overwhelmingly reported that these incredibly important spaces and structures gave them the skills and experience to engage academically and socially in school and beyond.

At present, HRE scholarship hones in on pedagogy and content, often in isolated programs, rather than how HRE might be diffused throughout a whole school or institution. A comprehensive approach to HRE pays attention to overall school *design* (ideological, physical, and structural) and is best supported when integrated into all aspects of school life. Fine et al. (1997) lament that "rarely have we had the pleasure of working with, studying, or even testifying for a truly 'integrated' school . . . one that self-consciously creates intellectual and social engagements across racial and ethnic groups" (p. 1). Schools that embrace HRE, like Prep and others mentioned in this book, endeavor to achieve this outcome. In the case of Prep, the school mission, vision, and Core Values serve as a compass by which to gauge school culture. Prep's structures and processes are not accidental or arbitrary; they are crucial mechanisms by which to move toward the realization of the school's mission. Other schools can follow suit and determine how to align their practices and processes with a more humane school culture that reflects HRE. The words of the students in this study show that such a context can lead to academic success and (re)socialization for even those students who have been marginalized and demoralized in mainstream schooling environments. Transformed student–teacher relationships are not sufficient; intentional institutional structures and processes are also indispensable.

CURRICULUM MATTERS

Thoughtful consideration of the academic curriculum is central to enacting a transformational HRE approach that dismisses deficit views of young people (Bartlett & García, 2011; Nieto, 2010) and instead embraces them as intellectually curious, passionate, capable of rigor, and concerned about and committed to changing the world. Prep students repeatedly emphasized how much they appreciated the theme-based, in-depth investigatory nature of their classes, which they felt engaged them in the learning process and also exposed them to new ways of thinking about what's going on around them and in the wider world, why, and how one might advocate for social change and justice amid these realities. This approach functions alongside and in tandem with the nonacademic structures at the school (i.e., Town Meetings/Quads, the Fairness Committee, and Advisory) to yield a comprehensive HRE-grounded curriculum that re-centers students' critical engagement with school.

The examples of such participatory spaces and approaches to curriculum design at the select NYC schools mentioned throughout the book illuminate how this may be envisioned at various schooling locales. Comprehensive curricula complement other aspects of school life to (re)socialize students academically by fostering critical participation and presumably provide these young people a channel from which to speak their minds, challenge preconceived perceptions about the world around them, and imagine alternatives for the future. This approach aligns with the myriad practices and goals of HRE outlined earlier and underscores the importance of intentionally including participatory practices in school reform, so that there is purposeful space for students to discuss, think about, and act upon issues that matter to them. At Prep, these spaces were pivotal sites for contestation, meaning-making, and questioning when the events of September 11th happened (see Hantzopoulos, 2004) and provided a template to deal with other issues and tragic events that seemingly may fall outside of the academic curriculum. For instance, in light of the horrific and tragic Charleston shootings and the murder of young Black men and women by the police, activists have called on educators to respond in the classroom (Simmons, 2015). Having participatory structures incorporated into the academic curriculum prevents schools and educators from making choices between discussing current events relevant to their lives and the traditional academic curriculum; instead, they are seamlessly connected and organically integrated.

The schools featured in this book also favor project-based assessment and oppose the overly prescriptive nature of standardized testing and standards-based reform. These schools are all lucky enough to be part of the New York Performance Standards Consortium and have a waiver from the high school Regents exams of New York State, with the exception of the English language arts Regents, which they must administer. Thus, their unique academic cultures are supported by project-based assessment to create a dynamic, inclusive model that inculcates democratic values and processes, allows room for student negotiation and engagement, and aligns with the goals of HRE. It is important to note that most current and former students at Prep reiterated that their classes were not textbook-based but drew from various sources and perspectives. Textbooks often are seen as sites for the construction of dominant cultural values, presenting a linear and singular view of history and thereby obfuscating the ways in which marginalized populations and ways of knowing have contributed to societies or resisted dominant ideologies (see Kaomea, 2000; Kuzmic, 2000). By working with and deconstructing these dominant narratives in their classes at Prep, students describe how they began to not only view "the world" differently, but also imagine new ways of thinking about the future. Related to this, students also described how they were involved in the process of analysis during their time at Prep; this included an examination of the self and one's role in society, so that historicized knowledge was (re)interpreted based on personal experience. According to Dauite (2000), this process allows students to envision multiple and alternative narratives for future action.

Overall, students described learning more (in terms of themselves, skills, and content knowledge) from project-based classes, and stated that this curricular approach made them more engaged in their education. This finding aligns with notions that standardized testing, which imposes a singular, historically bound "high-status" knowledge as absolute truth, does not always allow room for student negotiation and engagement. According to Deborah Meier (2000), it is more difficult for students to take responsibility for their own ideas when there is less "room" to present them. Prep students and alumni confirm this; they described being more engaged in school and being interested in school in ways they never had before. For students who previously have been unsuccessful or disengaged in/by school, a thematic and project-based curriculum may be a way to (re)socialize them, whereas retreating to a rigid standardized curriculum may exacerbate the situation. Overall, students in the Prep community suggest that the school's curricular approach intellectually invigorates and challenges them, and the same finding has emerged from analyses of other, similar schools (Tyner-Mullings, 2014).

Thus, fundamental to any discussion of how to enact HRE in schools is the role of testing and assessment in either inhibiting or fostering a culture of care, respect, critical questioning, and participation—and, by proxy, human dignity and worth. This is particularly instructive at this moment in time when even the federal government is starting to raise questions about the impact of high-stakes standardized testing on students' learning. While President Obama's recent proclamation that excessive testing has stripped the joy out of teaching and learning has not entirely changed policy despite NCLB being revised in December 2015, this rhetorical shift opens up discussions about alternative forms of assessment that may in fact instill joy, love, and rigor in the process of learning.

CONCLUDING THOUGHTS

As reflected in the stories and voices of the students and alumni highlighted throughout this book, students' experiences with HRE are mostly positive and transformative. Overall, young people who attend or attended Humanities Preparatory Academy feel that the school creates a comprehensive "curriculum" designed to give students numerous experiences with democratic participation (through building community and encouraging all members of that community to express opinions and exchange ideas) that help every member of the student body cultivate critical consciousness and a commitment to broader social change. Not only does this holistic curriculum and framework help (re)socialize students academically, but former and current students overwhelmingly feel that the school allows them to cultivate their "voice" and develop a platform for thinking about the world differently and more critically than they had before. The nature of this feedback suggests that Prep is an exemplar of HRE strategies that can be enacted in public schools.

There is no question, however, that attention must be paid to context, particularly as the HRE approaches at Prep and these other schools developed organically, internally; HRE approaches are, indeed, often "homegrown." While some of the structures and processes described in previous chapters are original and others were borrowed and adapted from other institutions, in all cases they continue to be tweaked and remade, evolving to meet the needs of the specific school population. HRE should not be rigidly imposed upon any school; HRE structures, processes, and practices should be dynamically integrated to fluidly embody the key principles of a holistic human rights approach.

Nonetheless, these schools offer an instructive source of inspiration for not only how HRE can be realized in urban settings, but also how HRE can serve as a counterpoint to contemporary educational policies and revitalize public schooling in the United States. While present educational policies narrowly focus on testing and discipline, despite evidence that these initiatives have only exacerbated inequities in schooling and even know the federal government admitting that they are excessive, I posit that mainstreaming HRE offers hope that public schools can work toward higher levels of educational access and attainment. In this sense, HRE fosters human rights learning and also serves as a mechanism to include students who have been demoralized and marginalized by previous schooling experiences. The acknowledgment of these possibilities does not negate the reality that micro, macro, systemic, and societal forces present challenges for HRE in schools, and, in fact, may render some of the utopic aims of HRE impossible. Yet, it is my hope that more public schools will begin to engage and grapple with these challenges to move the project of HRE in new directions, understanding that the endeavor requires constant conscious reflexive work and that the work is always partial and never complete.

As I conclude, I think about these humanizing and dignified spaces for young people and the adults who work with them. I recently visited Harvest Collegiate and Lyons Community School, both newly admitted to the Consortium,[1] to participate in roundtables where students presented their truly impressive work. As I roam the halls of these schools, as well as others, I am always struck by and make note of the artwork and posters that adorn the hallways. Bulletin boards devoted to the Black Lives Matter movement, information about the school-to-prison pipeline, and environmental awareness, sustainability, and action are commonplace, alongside vibrant murals and original student work. Even though these schools are often in otherwise run-down physical spaces, these artifacts exemplify a commitment to centering the voices, hopes, and dreams of the young people who attend them, bringing these places to life in a way that a stately brand-new building might fall short.

I also remember the first time I entered Prep, back in 1997, as a prospective teacher, thinking that I had never seen a school space that so vibrantly and passionately embraced student lives. I was impressed with what I saw there instructionally, and it was clear that this was an institution committed to project-based learning and incorporating democratic practices. I visited a Town Meeting where students and a guest speaker from the New York Public Interest Group discussed issues of environmental racism; observed an American History class conversation about women's rights movements; participated in a small Advisory discussion about the Town Meeting; and then had a 1-hour conversation with the principal about his vision for the school and my own background and experiences. But most important, it was the students' enthusiasm for attending the school that intrigued me and compelled me to accept a position there. Years later, in the late spring of 2005, I ran into eight former students in a 2-week period. Each one shared stories about their lives post-Prep, inspiring me to embark upon this research project.

I also think about a visit to Prep, well after I had taught there, to talk on a "Career Panel" about my job as a professor. When I arrived that morning, all of the guests clustered in Prep Central, greeted by student "ambassadors" who directed us so that each Quad would have at least six guests. The students ushered us over to the couches to wait and made sure that we took full advantage of the spread of croissants, fruit, muffins, and coffee they had ordered for us. While I was very familiar with the school and knew many of the students, one guest, an art director and photographer, turned to me and expressed how amazed he was at the level of natural conviviality among these high school students and adults. He described to another guest, a lawyer, his rural Illinois high school experience of metal detectors and segregated students and adults. She noted that her Brooklyn high school had succumbed to the same fate.

Students at Prep and young people at other HRE-centric schools are, in many ways, just like students in the traditional mainstream schools these guests were recalling with regret. What is strikingly different, however, are the schools they attend. Each time I visit Prep, Urban Academy, the James Baldwin School, and other schools with similar aims and practices, I am inspired and humbled by the work of those teachers and students trying to create spaces of hope for New York City youth. Their commitments to inquiry, constructive critique, growth, and continual transformation are impressive and inspiring, and show clearly that schools can be vibrant sites of teaching and learning. It is my hope that this book may contribute to informing the possible in schools, being in dialogue with parallel efforts and, also where this has not been imagined, sparking deeper conversations about how and why we need to embark upon more humane and dignified urban educational reform efforts.

Demographic Data of Current and Former Prep Students Interviewed

Demographic Data of Current Students Interviewed[1]

Name	Gender	Grade	Race/Ethnicity	Transfer
Ana	F	9th	Latina	N
Joshua	M	9th	African American	N
Epiphany	F	9th	Latina	N
Vivian	F	12th	African American	N
Magdalena	F	12th	Latina	N
Victor	M	12th	Puerto Rican	Y

Demographic Data of Former Students Interviewed

Name	Gender	Race/Ethnicity	Vocation/Education	Transfer
Alejo	M	Latino	College Student; Radio Shack	Y
Alek	M	White/ South Asian	Military (Graduated Johns Hopkins)	Y
Amelia	F	African American	College Student (Knox)	N
Monique	F	African American	College (Middlebury)	N
Marianna	F	African American	Some college (Bard), looking for work	Y
Dalia	F	Arab	College (Pace); cosmetics; film	Y
Sammy	M	White	College (Purchase)	Y
Kevin	M	Latino	College (Middlebury)	N
Isabel	F	Latina	College (Fordham)	N
Pedro	M	Latino	College (John Jay)	N

1. Information regarding gender and race/ethnicity is based on how students self-identify.

Reneka	F	African	College (Dillard)	N
Jenkins	M	African American	Working (Will go to college next year)	N
Isaiah	M	White	College (CCNY)	Y
Deena	F	Jewish/ West Indian	College (Wells)	N
Luis	M	Latino	College (Hunter)	N
Katerina	F	White	Doula	Y
Erin	F	Jamaican	College (Arizona)	N
Lisa	F	Latina	College (hunter)	Y
Shawn	M	African American	College (Albany)	N
Rebecca	F	Jamaican/ Liberian	College (Villanova)	N
Queenia	F	African American	Bank Teller	N

Demographic Data of Current Students in Focus Groups

FOCUS GROUP 1

Name	Gender	Race/Ethnicity	Grade	Transfer
Stacy	F	West Indian	12th	No
Jennifer	F	African	12th	No
Sebastien	F	African American	12th	No

FOCUS GROUP 2

Name	Gender	Race/Ethnicity	Grade	Transfer
Chakasia	F	African American/ Latina	10th	Yes
Henry	M	African American	11th	Yes
Saleema	F	African American	12th	No

FOCUS GROUP 3

Name	Gender	Race/Ethnicity	Grade	Transfer
Jonathan	M	White	10th	Yes and no
Javier	M	Latino	10th	No
Bonita	F	Latina	11th	No
Minerva	F	Latina	11th	No
Robin	F	African American	10th	Yes
Vaughn	M	Asian/ Latino	11th	No

FOCUS GROUP 4

Name	Gender	Race/Ethnicity	Grade	Transfer
Matthew	M	West Indian	12th	No
Mattias	M	West Indian	12th	No
Paul	M	Latino	12th	Yes
Sandra	F	African American	12th	Yes

Genna	F	Asian	12th	Yes
Richie	M	West Indian	12th	Yes

FOCUS GROUP 5

Name	Gender	Race/Ethnicity	Grade	Transfer
Selma	F	Arab	10th	Yes
Giancarlo	F	Latino	11th	No
Zack	M	White	11th	Yes
Serena	F	Latina	11th	Yes
Faye	F	Latina	11th	Yes

Humanities Preparatory Academy Mission Statement (1997)

It is our mission to provide a philosophical and practical education for all students, an education that features creativity and inquiry, encourages habitual reading and productivity, as well as self-reflection and original thought. We agree with Socrates that the "unexamined life is not worth living," and it is our desire to prepare students to live thoughtful and meaningful lives. We are committed to inspiring the love of learning in our students.

This mission can best be accomplished in a school that is a democratic community. As a democratic community, we strive to exemplify the values of democracy: mutual respect, cooperation, empathy, the love of humankind, justice for all, and service to the world.

Humanities Preparatory Academy is college preparatory. Our curriculum and pedagogy prepare students for the rigors of college work and motivate them to desire and plan for a higher education. In preparing students for college we believe that we move students toward higher levels of intellectual engagement while they are in high school.

It is our mission, as well, at Humanities Preparatory Academy, to provide a haven for students who have previously experienced school as unresponsive to their needs as individuals. We wish for all students to find their voice and to speak knowledgeably and thoughtfully on issues that concern their school, their world. We aid students in this endeavor by personalizing our learning situations, by democratizing and humanizing the school environment, and by creating a "talking culture," an atmosphere of informal intellectual discourse among students and faculty.

In order to achieve this, we intend . . .

- to restore a true understanding of the First Amendment: that freedom of expression is the highest democratic right and must be therefore taken seriously, and that democracy can only continue if opinions are based on evidence and meaningful thought;

- to encourage students to become passionate thinkers, seekers of truth and beauty, advocates for justice;

- to create an environment in which individuality is respected and cherished, an environment in which human beings are valued for the content of their character and the quality of their thought;

- to address the problem of student cynicism through promoting intellectual behaviors which lead to students' discovery of their own humanity and the value of human life, human feeling, human culture, human history, and the human endeavor;

- to promote an ongoing dialogue about the educational process, and to create an atmosphere of mutual intellectual and artistic endeavor in which students and teachers learn from each other;

- to cultivate the natural idealism of youth through promoting and honoring community work, and to acknowledge and engage the vital interdependency of the practical and the philosophical by creating meaningful external learning situations in the community at large;

- to advocate for peace and non-violence through an understanding of history, modeling respect and mutual esteem, and actively exploring and promoting alternatives to hurtful conflict in the realms of both interpersonal and political life;

- to provide moral alternatives and to help students become morally sensitive people, and to establish the connections between the academic disciplines and moral action, the connections between learning and community, thereby creating a just community in our school; and

- to employ the best progressive principles of education, to promote emotional as well as intellectual development, and to cultivate the various learning styles and intelligences present in all students. To this effect, we advocate that depth of inquiry, not coverage of material, guide classroom instruction.

Notes

Chapter 1

1. For example, in New York State, Governor Cuomo has proposed that the bulk of teacher evaluation be based on student performance on state high-stakes tests (see Decker, 2015). However, as of December 2015, the Governor has reconsidered this position given the push back from parents and families.

2. See Neil (2015) for an updated list of these incidents.

Chapter 2

1. ICOPE and Dignity in Schools Campaigns, for example.

2. See www.ohchr.org/EN/Issues/Education/Training/WPHRE/FirstPhase/Pages/NationalFocal.aspx for a partial list of nations that reference human rights in their national policies.

Chapter 3

1. All names have been changed in this book.

2. In 1996–97, students, parents, and teachers rallied to have Humanities Prep become autonomous as a means of ensuring that it remain intact. Humanities Prep was sponsored by New Visions for Public School in an early initiative to create new small schools throughout the city (see Hantzopoulos & Tyner-Mullings, 2012).

3. Prep is one of 28 schools that received a partial waiver from the Regents in 2002 and are allowed to implement performance-based assessment tasks for graduation in lieu of Regents exams.

4. NYC students are guaranteed a spot at their local "zoned" school, determined by their home address.

Chapter 5

1. Alumni Day is an annual event where former students are invited back to the school to speak to students in Town Meeting and Advisory about their experiences

post-Prep. At the end of the day, alumni debrief with staff about "What should Prep keep?" and "What should Prep change or improve upon?"

Chapter 6

1. At this time, Consortium school students are required to complete only the English language arts Regents; they complete project-based assessment tasks in English, math, history, and science.

2. This activity was inspired by the Rethinking Schools curriculum, "The Line Between Us" (see Bigelow, 2006).

Chapter 7

1. As Prep grew in size, it was no longer feasible to meet weekly as a whole-school community, so schoolwide Town Meetings were replaced with weekly "Quad" meetings. Quads are four rotating Advisories that meet weekly for the same purposes as previous Town Meetings. Following each rotation, the whole school comes together for one Town Meeting, after which the Quad rotation schedule resumes.

2. Restorative justice models focus more on the relationships among "victims" and "violators," as opposed to retributive justice, which emphasizes interpretation of strict legal code. Moreover, restorative justice specifically aims to restore harmony in the community.

Chapter 8

1. Taina, at the end of her sophomore year, moved to Florida with her family. She was so dissatisfied with her school there that she came back to New York on her own to enroll at Prep for the rest of her junior year and all of her senior year.

Chapter 9

1. In June 2014, the New York State Commissioner granted the Consortium waiver to 11 NYC public schools. Many of these schools had waited up to 8 years to be included in this variance, which allows them to administer project-based assessment tasks instead of Regents exams in all subject areas but English language arts.

References

Abrams, L. M., Pedulla, J. J., & Madaus, G. F. (2003). Views from the classroom: Teachers' opinions of statewide testing programs. *Theory into Practice*, 42(1), 18–29.

Abu-Lughod, L. (2010). The active social life of "Muslim women's rights": A plea for ethnography, not polemic, with cases from Egypt and Palestine. *Journal of Middle East Women's Studies*, 6(1), 1–44.

Adichie, C. (2013). The danger of a single story. Retrieved from www.ted.com/talks/ chimamanda_adichie_the_danger_of_a_single_story/transcript?language=en

Advancement Project, Education Law Center, FairTest, The Forum for Education and Democracy, Juvenile Law Center, & NAACP Legal Defense and Educational Fund, Inc. (2011). *Federal policy, ESEA re-authorization, and the school-to-prison pipeline.* Open Society Foundations. Retrieved from b.3cdn.net/ advancement/ceb35d4874b0ffde10_ubm6baeap.pdf

Advocates for Children. (2002). *Pushing out at-risk students: An analysis of high school discharge figures.* Retrieved from www.advocatesforchildren.org/sites/ default/files/library/pushing_out_2002.pdf?pt=1

American Civil Liberties Union. (2010). ACLU lawsuit challenges abusive police practices in New York City schools. Retrieved from www.aclu.org/racial-justice/ aclu-lawsuit-challenges-abusive-police-practices-new-york-city-schools

American Federation of Teachers Racial Justice Task Force (2015). Reclaiming the promise of racial equity: In education, economics, and our criminal justice system. Retrieved from www.aft.org

Amnesty International. (2012). *Guidelines for human rights friendly schools.* Human Rights Friendly School Project. London, UK: Amnesty International. Retrieved from www.amnesty.org/en/human-rights-education/human-rights-friendly-schools/

Amrein, A. T., & Berliner, D. C. (2003). The effects of high-stakes testing on student motivation and learning. *Educational Leadership*, 60(5), 32–33.

Andreopoulos, G. J., & Claude, R. P. (Eds.). (1997). *Human rights education for the twenty-first century.* Philadelphia: University of Pennsylvania Press.

Antrop-Gonzalez, R. (2011). *Schools as radical sanctuaries: Decolonizing urban education through the eyes of youth of color.* Charlotte, NC: Information Age.

Antrop-Gonzalez, R., & De Jesús, A. (2005). Toward a theory of critical care in urban small school reform: Examining structures and pedagogies of caring in two Latino community-based schools. *International Journal of Qualitative Studies in Education*, 19(4), 409–433.

Antrop-Gonzalez, R., & de Jesús, A. (2007). Breathing life into small school reform: Advocating for critical care in small schools of color. In B. Franklin &

G. McCulloch (Eds.), *The death of the comprehensive high school? Historical, contemporary, and comparative perspectives* (pp. 73–92). New York, NY: Palgrave Macmillan.

Anyon, J. (1997). *Ghetto schooling: A political economy of urban educational reform.* New York, NY: Teachers College Press.

Anyon, J. Dumas, M., Linville, D., Nolan, K., Perez, M., Tuck, E., & Weiss, J. (2009). *Theory and educational research: Toward critical social explanation.* New York: Routledge.

Apple, M. (2005). Are markets in education democratic? Neoliberal globalism, vouchers and the politics of choice. In M. Singh, J. Kenway, & M. Apple (Eds.), *Globalizing education* (pp. 209–230). New York, NY: Peter Lang.

Apple, M. W., & Beane, J. A. (Eds.). (2007). *Democratic schools* (2nd ed.). Alexandria, VA: Association for Supervision and Curriculum Development.

APSIDES. (2011). *Education for human rights: Young people talking.* Paris, France: UNESCO.

Arbuthnot, K. (2011). *Filling in the blanks: Understanding the Black/White achievement gap.* Charlotte, NC: Information Age.

Au, W. (2009). Unequal by design: High-Stakes Testing and the Standardization of inequality. New York: Routledge.

Bajaj, M. (2008). Critical peace education. In M. Bajaj (Ed.), *Encyclopedia of peace education* (pp. 135–146). Charlotte, NC: Information Age.

Bajaj, M. (2009). Why context matters: Understanding the material conditions of school-based caring in Zambia. *International Journal of Qualitative Studies in Education, 22*(4), 379–398.

Bajaj, M. (2011). Human rights education: Ideology, location, and approaches. *Human Rights Quarterly, 33*(2), 481–508.

Bajaj, M. (2012). *Schooling for social change: The rise and impact of human rights education in India.* New York & London: Continuum.

Bajaj, M., & Brantmeier, E. J. (2011). "Introduction to the Special Issue of the Journal of Peace Education on the Politics, Possibilities and Praxis of a Critical Peace Education," *Journal of Peace Education, 8*(3), 221–224.

Banks, J. (2009). Human rights, diversity, and citizenship education. *The Educational Forum, 73*, 100–110.

Bar-Tal, D. (2002). The elusive nature of peace education. In G. Salomon & B. Nevo (Eds.), *Peace education: The concept, principles and practice in the world* (pp. 27–36). Mahwah, NJ: Erlbaum.

Bartlett, L. (2005). Dialogue, knowledge, and teacher–student relations: Freirean pedagogy in theory and practice. *Comparative Education Review, 49*(3), 1–21.

Bartlett, L., & García, O. (2011). *Additive schooling in subtractive times: Bilingual education and Dominican immigrant youth in the Heights.* Nashville, TN: Vanderbilt University Press.

Bartlett, L., & Koyama, J. (2012). Additive schooling: A critical small school for Latino youth. In M. Hantzopoulos & A. Tyner-Mullings (Eds.), *Critical small schools: Beyond privatization in New York City urban educational reform* (pp. 79–102). Charlotte, NC: Information Age.

Baxi, U. (1997). The promise of the third millennium? In G. J. Andreopoulos & R. P. Claude (Eds.), *Human rights education for the twenty-first century* (pp. 142–154). Philadelphia, PA: University of Philadelphia Press.

Belenky, M. F., Clinchy, B. M., Goldberger, N. R., & Tarule, J. M. (1986). *Women's ways of knowing: The development of self, voice, and mind.* New York, NY: Basic Books.

Berliner, D. C., & Biddle, B. J. (1995). *The manufactured crisis: Myths, fraud, and the attack on America's public schools.* New York, NY: Basic Books.

Berliner, D., & Glass, G. (2014). *50 myths and lies that threaten America's public schools: The real crisis in education.* New York, NY: Teachers College Press.

Bigelow, B. (2006). *The line between us: Teaching about the border and Mexican immigration.* Milwaukee, WI: Rethinking Schools.

Boaler, J. (2006). Opening Their Ideas: How a de-tracked math approach promoted respect, responsibility and high achievement. *Theory into Practice, 45*(1), 40–46.

Bowditch, C. (1993). Getting rid of troublemakers: High school disciplinary procedures and the production of dropouts. *Social Problems, 40,* 493–509.

Bridgeland, J., Dilulio, J., & Balfanz, R. (2009). The high school dropout problem: Perspectives of teachers and principals. *Education Digest: Essential Readings Condensed for Quick Review, 75*(3), 20–26.

Bridgeland, J., Dilulio, J., & Morison, K. (2006). *The silent epidemic: Perspectives from high school dropouts.* Retrieved from docs.gatesfoundation.org/Documents/TheSilentEpidemic3-06Final.pdf

Burke, R. (2006). The compelling dialogue of freedom: Human rights at the Bandung Conference. *Human Rights Quarterly, 28*(4), 947–965.

Burris, C. C., Heubert, J., & Levin, H. (2006). Accelerating mathematics achievement using heterogeneous grouping. *American Educational Research Journal 43*(1), 103–134.

Burris, C.C. & Wellner, K. (2005). Closing the achievement gap by detracking. Phi *Delta Kappan, 86*(8), 594–598.

Cardenas, S. (2005). Constructing rights? Human rights education and the state. *International Political Science Review, 26*(4), 363–379.

Center for Research on Educational Outcomes. (2009). *Multiple choice: Charter school performance in 16 states.* Stanford, CA: Stanford University. Retrieved from credo.stanford.edu/reports/MULTIPLE_CHOICE_CREDO.pdf

Christie, C. A., Jolivette, K., & Nelson, C. M. (2007). School characteristics related to high school dropout rates. *Remedial and Special Education, 28,* 325–339.

Claude, R. P. (2011). A letter to my colleagues, students, and readers of Human Rights Quarterly. *Human Rights Quarterly, 33,* 578–585.

Crenshaw, K. (2015). Black girls matter: Pushed out, overpoliced and underprotected. African American Policy Forum. Retrieved from www.aapf.org/recent/2014/12/coming-soon-blackgirlsmatter-pushed-out-overpoliced-and-underprotected

D'Agastino, B. (2012). *The middle class fights back: How progressive movements can restore democracy in America.* New York, NY: ABC-CLIO.

Danesh, H. B. (2006). Towards an integrative theory of peace education. *Journal of Peace Education, 3*(1), 55–78.

Dauite, C. (2000). Narrative Sites for youth's construction of social consciousness. In L. Weis & M. Fine, *Construction sites: Excavating race, class, and gender among urban youth* (pp. 211–234). New York, NY: Teachers College Press.

Decker, G. (2015). States evaluation proposal prompts frustration, dissent among Regents. Chalkbeat. Retrieved from http://ny.chalkbeat.org/2015/05/19/regents-register-dissent-on-evaluation-proposal/#.VjZYoKIViGg

De Jesús, A. (2003). Here it's more like your house: The proliferation of authentic caring as school reform at El Puente Academy for Peace and Justice. In B. Rubin & E. Silva (Eds.), *Critical voices: Students living school reform* (pp. 132–150). London, UK: Routledge Falmer.

De Jesús, A. (2012). Authentic caring and community driven reform: The case of El Puente Academy for Peace and Justice. In M. Hantzopoulos & A. Tyner-Mullings (Eds.), *Critical small schools: Beyond privatization in New York City urban educational reform* (pp. 63–78). Charlotte, NC: Information Age.

Diaz-Soto, L. (2005). How can we teach peace when we are so outraged? A call for critical peace education. *Taboo: The Journal of Culture and Education, 9*(2), 91–96.

Ellsworth, E. (1989). Why doesn't this feel empowering? Working through repressive myths of critical pedagogy. *Harvard Educational Review, 59*(3), 297–324.

Eubanks, E., Parish, R., & Smith, D. (1997). Changing the discourse in schools. In P. Hall (Ed.), *Race, ethnicity, and multiculturalism: Policy and practice.* New York, NY: Routledge.

Fabricant, M., & Fine, M. (2012). *Charter schools and the corporate makeover of public education: What's at stake?* New York, NY: Teachers College Press.

Fergusen, A. (2001). *Bad boys: Public schools in the making of Black masculinity.* Ann Arbor, MI: University of Michigan Press.

Fine, M. (1991). *Framing dropouts: Notes on the politics of an urban high school.* Albany, NY: State University of New York Press.

Fine, M., Weis, L., & Powell, L. (1997). Communities of difference: A critical look at desegregated spaces created for and by youth. *Harvard Educational Review, 67*(2), 247–284.

Fine, M. & Ruglis, J. (2009). Circuits and consequences of dispossession: The racialized and classed realignment of the public sphere for U.S. youth. *Transforming Anthropology, 17*(1), 20–33.

Flowers, N. (2000). *The human rights education handbook: Effective practices for learning, action, and change.* Minneapolis, MN: Human Rights Resource Center, University of Minnesota.

Flowers, N. (2004). What is human rights education? In V. Georgi & M. Seberich (Eds.), *International perspectives in human rights education.* Hamburg, Germany: Bertelsmann Foundation Press. Retrieved from: http://www.hrea.org/erc/Library/curriculum_methodology/flowers03.pdf

Foote, M. (2012). Freedom from high stakes testing: A formula for small school success. In M. Hantzopoulos & A. Tyner-Mullings (Eds.), *Critical small schools: Beyond privatization in New York City urban educational reform* (pp. 121–133). Charlotte, NC: Information Age.

Freire, P. (2003). *The pedagogy of the oppressed.* New York, NY: Continuum. (Original work published 1972)

Futrell, M. H., & Rotberg, I. C. (2002). Predictable casualties: Do we risk leaving more children behind? *Education Week, 22*(5), 34–48.

Galtung, J. (2008). Form and content in peace education. In M. Bajaj (Ed.), *Encyclopedia of peace education* (pp. 49–58). Charlotte, NC: Information Age.

García, O., Flores, N., & Woodley, H. (2012). Transgressing monolingualism and bilingual dualities: Translanguaging pedagogies. In A. Yiakoumetti (Ed.), *Harnessing linguistic variation to improve education* (pp. 45–75). Bern, Switzerland: Peter Lang.

Gilligan, C. (1982). *In a different voice: Psychological theory and women's development.* Cambridge, MA: Harvard University Press.

Giroux, H., & Penna, A. (1983). Social education in the classroom: The dynamics of the hidden curriculum. In H. Giroux & D. Purpel (Eds.), *The hidden curriculum and moral education* (pp. 100–121). Berkeley, CA: McCutchan.

Glendon, M. (2001). *A world made new: Eleanor Roosevelt and the Universal Declaration of Human Rights.* New York, NY: Random House.

Gore, J. (1992). What can we do for you! What can "we" do for "you"? Struggling over empowerment in critical and feminist pedagogy. In. J. Gore & C. Luke (Eds.), *Feminisms and pedagogies* (pp. 54–73). New York, NY: Routledge.

Grant, C., & Gibson, M. (2013). The path of social justice: A human rights history of social justice education. *Equity and Excellence in Education, 46*(1), 81–99.

Greene, M. (1986). In search of a critical pedagogy. *Harvard Educational Review, 56*(4), 427–441.

Haavelsrud, M. (2008). Conceptual perspectives in peace education. In M. Bajaj (Ed.), *Encyclopedia of peace education* (pp. 50–59). Charlotte, NC: Information Age.

Hagopian, J. (2014). *More than a score: The new uprising against high stakes testing.* Boston, MA: Haymarket.

Hannah-Jones, N. (2015). The continuing reality of segregated schools. New York Times magazine. Retrieved from http://www.nytimes.com/2015/07/31/magazine/the-continuing-reality-of-segregated-schools.html?_r=0

Hantzopoulos, M. (2004). The impact of standardized testing on the deliverance of post-conflict education: A case study of one New York City high school. *Education in Emergencies* [a Columbia University graduate student publication]. Columbia University, New York.

Hantzopoulos, M. (2006). Deepening democracy. *Rethinking Schools, 21*(1). Retrieved from www.rethinkingschools.org/restrict.asp?path=archive/21_01/demo211.shtml

Hantzopoulos, M. (2009). Transformative schooling in restrictive times: The critical small schools movement and standards-based reform in the United States. In F. Vavrus & L. Bartlett (Eds.), *Comparatively knowing: Vertical case study research in comparative and development education* (pp. 111–126). New York, NY: Palgrave.

Hantzopoulos, M. (2011a). Deepening democracy: How one school's fairness committee offers an alternative to "discipline." Reprinted with permission from *Rethinking Schools* in *Schools: Studies in Education, 8*(1), 112–116.

Hantzopoulos, M. (2011b). Institutionalizing critical peace education in public schools: A case for comprehensive implementation. *Journal of Peace Education, 8*(3), 225–242.

Hantzopoulos, M. (2012a). Human rights education as public school reform. *Peace Review: A Journal of Social Justice, 24,* 36–45.

Hantzopoulos, M. (2012b). When cultures collide: Students' successes and challenges as transformative change agents within and beyond a democratic school. In M. Hantzopoulos & A. Tyner-Mullings (Eds.), *Critical small schools: Beyond privatization in New York City urban educational reform* (pp. 189–212). Charlotte, NC: Information Age.

Hantzopoulos, M. (2013). The possibilities of restorative justice in US public schools: A case study of the fairness committee at a small NYC high school. *The Prevention Researcher, 20*(1), 7–10.

Hantzopoulos, M., & Shirazi, R. (2014). Securing the state through the production of "global" citizens: Analyzing neoliberal educational reforms in Jordan and the United States through the production of global citizens. *Policy Futures in Education, 12*(3), 370–386.

Hantzopoulos, M., & Tyner-Mullings, A. (2012). Introduction. *Critical small schools: Beyond privatization in New York City urban educational reform* (pp. xxv–xliv). Charlotte, NC: Information Age.

Harris, I. (2008). History of peace education. In M. Bajaj (Ed.), *Encyclopedia of peace education* (pp. 15–23). Charlotte, NC: Information Age.

Harris, I., & Morrison, M. (2003). *Peace education.* Jefferson, NC: McFarland.

Hart, D., Donnelly, T., Youniss, J., & Atkins, R. (2007). High school community service as a predictor of adult voting and volunteering. *American Educational Research Journal, 44*(1), 161–196.

Haywood, F. (2002, June 19). Middle school dropout rate up. *Boston Herald*, p. 3.

Herszenhorn, D. (2006, April 14). Students to get no warning before searches. *New York Times*. Retrieved from www.nytimes.com/2006/04/14/education/14educ.html?_r=0

Horn, C. (2003). High-stakes testing and students: Stopping or perpetuating a cycle of failure. *Theory into Practice, 42*(1), 30–41.

Horn, I. S. (2006). Lessons learned from detracked mathematics departments. *Theory into Practice, 45*(1), 72–81.

Howard, R. E. (1997/98). Human rights and the culture wars: Globalization and the universality of human rights. *International Journal, 53*(1), 94–112.

Hursh, D. (2007). Assessing no child left behind and the rise of neoliberal education policies. *American Educational Research Journal, 44*(3), 493–518.

Independent Commission on Public Education. (2012). *Getting out from under: A human rights alternative to the corporate model of public education in New York City.* New York, NY: ICOPE.

Ishay, M. (2004). *The history of human rights: From ancient times to the globalization era.* Berkeley, CA: University of California Press.

Kaomea, J. (2000). A curriculum of aloha? Colonialism and tourism in Hawaii's elementary textbooks. *Curriculum Inquiry, 30*(3), 319–344.

Karp, S. (2006). Band-aids or bulldozers. *Rethinking Schools, 20*(3), 26–29.

Kati, K., & Gjedia, R. (2003). *Educating the next generation: Incorporating human rights education in the public school system.* Minneapolis, MN: New Tactics in Human Rights Project.

Katsyianis, A., Zhang, D., Ryan, J., & Jones, J. (2007). High stakes testing and students with disabilities: Challenges and promises. *Journal of Disability Policy Studies, 8*(3), 160–167.

Knight, F. (2005). The Haitian revolution and the notion of human rights. *Journal of the Historical Society, 3*, 391–416.

Knoester, M. (2012). *Democratic education in practice: Inside the Mission Hill School.* New York, NY: Teachers College Press.

Koenig, S. (1997). Foreword. In G. J. Andreopoulos & R. P. Claude (Eds.), *Human rights education for the twenty-first century* (pp. xiii–xvii). Philadelphia, PA: University of Pennsylvania Press.

Kucsera, J. (with Orfield, G). (2014). New York State's extreme school segregation: Inequality, inaction and a damaged future. *The Civil Rights Project.* Retrieved from civilrightsproject.ucla.edu/research/k-12-education/integration-and-diversity/ny-norflet-report-placeholder/Kucsera-New-York-Extreme-Segregation-2014.pdf

Kumashiro, K. (2008). *The seduction of common sense: How the right has framed the debate on America's schools.* New York, NY: Teachers College Press.

Kuzmic, J. (2000). Textbooks, knowledge and masculinity: Examining patriarchy from within. In N. Lesko (Ed.), *Masculinities at school* (pp. 105–126). Thousand Oaks, CA: Sage.

Ladson-Billings, G. (2006). From the achievement gap to the educational debt: Understanding Achievement in US schools. *Educational Researcher, 35*(7), 3–12.

Lee, T., Cornell, D., Gregory, A., & Fan, X. (2011). High suspension schools and dropout rates for Black and White students. *Education and the Treatment of Children, 35,* 167–192.

Lipman, P. (2011) *The new political economy of urban education: Neoliberalism, race, and the right to the city.* New York, NY: Routledge.

MacKinnon, C. (1993). Crimes of war, crimes of peace. In S. Shute & S. Hurely (Eds.), *On human rights: The Oxford Amnesty lectures 1993* (pp. 83–110). New York, NY: Basic Books.

Mamdani, M. (2009). The genocide myth. Interview with Joel Whitney. *Guernica.* Retrieved from www.guernicamag.com/interviews/the_genocide_myth/

Marchant, G. (2004). What is at stake with high stakes testing? *Ohio Journal of Science, 104*(2), 2–7.

Massad, J. (2002). Re-orienting desire: The gay international and the Arab world. *Public Culture, 14*(2), 361–385.

Maudaus, G. F., & Clarke, M. (2001). The adverse impact of high stakes testing on minority students: Evidence from 100 years of test data. In G. Orfield & M. Kornhaber (Eds.), *Raising standards or raising barriers? Inequality and high stakes testing in public education* (pp. 2–49). New York, NY: Century Foundation.

McCarty, T. (2010). Enduring inequities, imagined futures: Circulating policy discourses and dilemmas in Anthropology of Education. *Anthropology and Education Quarterly, 43*(1), 1–12.

McGinn, N. F. (1996). Education, democratization, and globalization: A challenge for comparative education. *Comparative Education Review, 40*(4), 341–357.

McNeil, L. (2005). Faking equity: High-stakes testing and the education of Latino youth. In A. Valenzuela (Ed.), *Leaving children behind: How "Texas-style" accountability fails Latino youth* (pp. 57–111). Albany, NY: State University of New York Press.

McNeil, L. M., Coppola, E., Radigan, J., & Vazquez-Heilig, J. (2011). Avoidable losses: High stakes accountability and the dropout crisis. *Education Policy Archives, 16*(3), 1–48.

Meier, D. (2000). Educating for a democracy. In J. Cohn & J. Rogers (Eds.), *Will standards save public education?* Boston, MA: Beacon Press.

Menken, K. (2008). *English learners left behind: Standardized testing as language policy.* Clevedon, New Zealand: Multilingual Matters.

Metijies, G. (1997). Human rights education as empowerment: Reflections on pedagogy. In G. J. Andreopoulos & R. P. Claude (Eds.), *Human rights education for the twenty-first century* (pp.64–79). Philadelphia, PA: University of Pennsylvania Press.

Milner, H. R. (2013). *Analyzing poverty, learning, and teaching through a critical race theory lens. Review of Research in Education, 37*(1), 1–53. Retrieved from rre.sagepub.com/content/37/1/1.full.pdf+html?ijkey=NZHbxRKYQYBfs& keytype=ref&siteid=sprre

Monahan, R. (2010, February 4). Queens girl Alexa Gonzalez hauled out of school handcuffed after getting caught doodling on desk. *Newsday*. Retrieved from www.newsdaynews.com

Mower, A. G. (1979). *The United States, the United Nations, and human rights: The Eleanor Roosevelt and Jimmy Carter eras*. Westport, CT: Greenwood.

National Economics and Social Rights Initiative (NESRI). (2007). *Deprived of dignity: Degrading treatment and abusive discipline in New York City & Los Angeles public schools*. New York, NY: Author.

National School Climate Council. (2015, May 5). School climate and pro-social educational improvement: Essential goals and processes that support student success for all. *Teachers College Record*. Retrieved from schoolclimate.org/climate/documents/Essential_dimensions_Prosocial_SC_Improvement_P_3-2015.pdf

Neil, M. (2015). Standardized test cheating in 37 states plus D.C. Jamaica Plain, MA: FairTest. Retrieved from fairtest.org/2013-Cheating-Report-PressRelease

New York Civil Liberties Union, Make the Road, & Annenberg Institute of School Reform. (2009). *Safety with dignity: Alternatives to the over-policing of schools*. New York, NY: New York Civil Liberties Union.

New York Performance Standards Consortium. (2008). Welcome. Retrieved from performanceassessment.org

New York Performance Standards Consortium. (2013). Educating for the 21st century: Data report on the New York performance standards consortium. Retrieved from www.nyclu.org/files/releases/testing_consortium_report.pdf

Nichols, S., & Berliner, D. (2007). *Collateral damage: How high-stakes testing corrupts America's schools*. Cambridge, MA: Harvard Education Press.

Nieto, S. (2010). *Language, culture, and teaching: Critical perspectives for a new century* (2nd ed.). New York, NY: Routledge.

Noddings, N. (1992). *The challenge to care in schools: An alternative approach to education*. New York, NY: Teachers College Press.

Oakes, J. (2005). *Keeping track: How schools structure inequality*. New Haven, CT: Yale University Press.

Oyler, C., & Becker, J. (1997). Teaching beyond the progressive–traditional dichotomy: Sharing authority and sharing vulnerability. *Curriculum Inquiry, 27*(4), 453–467.

People's Decade of Human Rights Education (PDHRE). (2014). PDHRE establishes regional and international learning institutions for human rights education. Retrieved from www.pdhre.org/ilihre.html

Ramirez, F. O., Suarez, D., & Meyer, J. W. (2006). The worldwide rise of human rights education. In A. Benavot & C. Braslavsky (Eds.), *School knowledge in comparative and historical perspective: Changing curricula in primary and secondary education* (pp. 35– 52). Hong Kong: Comparative Education Research Centre & Springer.

Ravitch, D. (2011). *The death and life of the great American school system: How testing and choice are undermining education*. New York, NY: Basic Books.

Ravitch, D. (2014). *The reign of error: The hoax of the privatization movement and the danger to America's public schools.* New York. NY: Knopf.

Reardon, B. (1988). *Comprehensive peace education.* New York, NY: Teachers College Press.

Reardon, B. (1996). *Educating for human dignity.* Philadelphia, PA: University of Pennsylvania Press.

Reardon, B. (2001). *Education for a culture of peace in a gender perspective.* Paris, France: UNESCO.

Rivera-McCutchen, R. (2012). Considering context: Exploring a small school's struggle to maintain its educational vision. In M. Hantzopoulos & A. Tyner-Mullings (Eds.), *Critical small schools: Beyond privatization in New York City urban educational reform* (pp. 21–39). Charlotte, NC: Information Age.

Rodriguez, L., & Conchas, G. (2008). *Small schools and urban youth: Using the power of school culture to engage students.* Thousand Oaks, CA: Sage.

Rothstein, R., Jacobsen, R., & Wilder, T. (2008, February 21). *Reassessing the achievement gap: Fully measuring what students should be taught in schools.* Campaign for Educational Equity. www.tc.columbia.edu/i/media/6573_Sum_Rpt_CEE.pdf

Rubin, B. (2006). Tracking and detracking: Debates, evidence and best practices for heterogeneous world. *Theory Into Practice, 45*(1), 4–14.

Rumberger, R. (2004). Why students drop out of school. In G. Orfield (Ed.), *Dropouts in America: Confronting the crisis* (pp. 131–155). Cambridge, MA: Harvard University Press.

Schniedewind, N. & Sapon-Shevin, M., (2012). *Educational courage: Resisting the ambush on public education.* Boston, MA: Beacon Press.

Sen, A. (1999). *Development as freedom* (pp. 227–248). Cambridge, England: Oxford University Press.

Shiller, J. (2012). City Prep: A Culture of Care in an Era of Data Driven Reform. In M. Hantzopoulos & A. Tyner-Mullings (Eds.). *Critical small schools: Moving beyond privatization in New York City public school reform* (pp. 3–20). Charlotte, NC: Information Age Publishing.

Simmons, D. (2015). How educators can respond to Charleston: Allow your students to reflect and act. Dare to be vulnerable. Teach empathy and love. *Medium.* Retrieved from medium.com/bright/how-educators-can-respond-to-charleston-366bce1b1d61

Suh, S., & Suh, J. (2007). Risk factors and levels of risk for high school dropouts. *Professional School Counseling, 10,* 297–306.

Sullivan, E. (2007). *Deprived of dignity: Degrading treatment and abusive discipline in New York City & Los Angeles public schools.* New York, NY: National Economic and Social Rights Initiative.

Taubman, P. (2013). *Educational revolution* [Occasional Paper Series]. New York, NY: Bank Street College of Education. Retrieved from www.bankstreet.edu/occasional-paper-series/27/part-i/educational-revolution/

Tibbits, F. (1996). On human dignity: A renewed call for human rights education. *Social Education, 60*(7), 428–431.

Tibbits, F. (2002). Understanding what we do: Emerging models for human rights education. *International Review of Education, 48*(3–4), 159–171.

Tibbits, F. (2008). Human rights education. In M. Bajaj (Ed.), *Encyclopedia of peace education* (pp. 99–108). Charlotte, NC: Information Age.

Tuck, E. (2012). *Urban youth and school push-out: Gateways, getaways, and the GED.* New York, NY: Routledge.

Tyner-Mullings, A. (2012). Redefining success: How CPESS students reached the goals that mattered. In M. Hantzopoulos & A. Tyner-Mullings (Eds.), *Critical small schools: Beyond privatization in New York City urban educational reform* (pp. 137–166). Charlotte, NC: Information Age.

Tyner-Mullings, A. (2014). *Enter the alternative school: Critical answers to questions in urban education.* New York, NY: Paradigm.

United Nations. (1948). *Universal declaration of human rights.* Retrieved from www.un.org/en/documents/udhr/

United Nations. (2012). *United Nations global education first initiative.* Retrieved from www.globaleducationfirst.org/about.html

Valenzuela, A. (1999). *Subtractive schooling: U.S.-Mexican Youth and the Politics of Caring.* Ithaca, NY: State University of New York Press.

Vazquez-Heilig, J., & Darling-Hammond, L. (2008). Accountability Texas-style: The progress and learning of urban minority students in a high-stakes testing context. *Educational Evaluation and Policy Analysis, 30*(2), 75–110.

Walker, E. (2012). *Building mathematics learning communities.* New York, NY: Teachers College Press.

Watkins, W. H. (Ed.). (2012). *The assault on public education: Confronting the politics of corporate school reform.* New York, NY: Teachers College Press.

West, C. (2004). *Democracy matters: Winning the fight against imperialism.* New York, NY: Penguin.

Winn, M. (2007). *Writing in rhythm: Spoken word poetry in urban classrooms.* New York, NY: Teachers College Press.

Wright, D. (2015). *Active learning: Social justice education and participatory action research.* New York, NY: Routledge.

Zembylas, M. (2011). Peace and human rights education: Dilemmas of compatibility and prospects for moving forward. *Quarterly Review of Comparative Education, 41*(4), 567–579.

Index

Urban Academy (New York City), 9, 37, 83–84, 100, 151

Valenzuela, A., 50, 55, 58, 61, 144
Values and awareness model of human rights education, 20
Vaughn (Prep student), 77, 78, 86, 154
Vazquez-Heilig, J., 2, 4
Victor (Prep student), 40–41, 43, 51, 56–57, 60, 76–77, 82, 87, 106, 116, 139, 153
Vivian (Prep student), 40, 41, 58–59, 69, 76, 91, 153

Walker, E., 111
Watkins, W. H., 6

Weis, L., 11, 68, 121, 125, 146–147
Weiss, J., 10
Wellner, K., 99
West, C., 23
Wilder, T., 108
Winn, M., 9, 61
Woodley, H., 55
World Wide Wrestling Federation, 135
Wright, D., 131
Youniss, J., 83

Zack (Prep student), 49, 54, 155
Zambia, 144
Zembylas, M., 18–19, 23–24
Zero-tolerance policies, 4–5, 64
Zhang, D., 4

About the Author

Maria Hantzopoulos is associate professor of education at Vassar College, where she is coordinator of the Adolescent Education Certification Program and a participating faculty member in the programs in International Studies, Urban Studies, and Women's Studies. Prior to Vassar, she taught and worked in New York City public schools for 13 years, served on several public school planning teams, and worked with a variety of established youth organizations. Dr. Hantzopoulos's work has appeared in a variety of peer-reviewed publications and she is coeditor, with Dr. Alia Tyner-Mullings, of *Critical Small Schools: Beyond Privatization in New York City Urban Educational Reform* (2012) and, with Dr. Monisha Bajaj, of *Peace Education: International Perspectives* (forthcoming). She was also the primary investigator for and recipient of the British Council/Social Science Research Council "Our Shared Past" Grant (along with four other co-investigators), which has culminated in the curriculum "Rethinking the Region: New Approaches to 9–12 U.S. Curriculum on MENA." She currently is conducting a research project, funded by the Spencer Foundation, documenting how schools transition from high-stakes testing to project-based assessment. Dr. Hantzopoulos went to public schools in Peabody, Massachusetts, before earning her BA magna cum laude from Boston University in history. She obtained her MA in social studies education and her doctorate in international educational development, with a specialization in peace education, from Teachers College, Columbia University.